Affairs of Poison True Crime's Deadliest Poisoners

Dylan Frost

Other Books By Dylan Frost

Shocking Celebrity Deaths and Murders

-

Shocking Celebrity Deaths and Murders Volume 2

-

Shocking Celebrity Deaths and Murders Volume 3

-

Last Meals - The Final Suppers of Serial Killers & Murderers

-

Jack the Ripper - A Smorgasbord of Suspects

-

Britain's Strangest True Crime Cases

-

Chilling True Crime Stories

-

Chilling True Crime Stories - Volume 2

-

Chilling True Crime Stories - Volume 3

-

Chilling True Crime Stories - Volume 4

Contents

6 - Chapter One - Cads & Bounders
27 - Chapter Two - She Seemed Like Such a Nice Old Lady
41 - Chapter Three - Poisoning Gangs
56 - Chapter Four - Black Widows
90 - Chapter Five - Medical Professional Poisoners
122 - Chapter Six - The Best (Or Should That Be Worst?) Of the Rest

CHAPTER ONE - CADS & BOUNDERS

Radford University's data suggested that only 7% of serial killers murdered their victims by means of poison. During the Middle Ages in Europe, poison became a popular method of assassination, particularly among the nobility and ruling class. The Italian Renaissance witnessed a surge in poison-related crimes, with several notorious figures using poison to secure power or eliminate political rivals. The Borgias, one of the most infamous Italian families, were strongly associated with poisonings, as they were suspected of poisoning numerous individuals to further their political interests.

A lot of famous poisoners in true crime history are women and we'll certainly get around to a great deal of those notorious females later on in the book. For this opening chapter though we'll focus on some of the most famous male poisoners. Your average serial killer does not use poison. They prefer to get their hands dirty - so to speak. It clearly would not have satisfied a Ted Bundy or Richard Ramirez to kill someone with poison. Poison, as far as serial killing goes, is what you might describe as a more refined sort of MO. It is generally (though not always) done by the sort of criminal who prefers not to resort to brute force or weapons. These killers are no less heartless because the end result, whether by arsenic or the axe, is the same but they often tend to be more 'well to do' people in social terms than your bog standard murderous maniac.

THOMAS GRIFFITHS WAINEWRIGHT was born in 1794. He tends to be known as Wainewright the Poisoner in true crime articles. Wainewright was an unusual candidate to be a serial killer because he had a good education, was an officer in the army, and then became an artist. He was a painter and literary critic who hobnobbed with the rich and famous. There was only one problem though. Wainewright developed expensive tastes and enjoyed a lavish lifestyle but he could never earn enough money to fund this. Well, given the title of this book, you probably won't be surpised to learn that Thomas Griffiths Wainewright eventually resorted to murder as a means to get his hands on the money he desperately craved.

In the end, Wainewright was racking up so many debts he had begun forging shares. In 1821 he married Eliza Frances Ward. Wainewright invited his uncle to come and stay with them but the relative died less than a year later - leaving his fortune to Thomas. It is believed that strychnine was used in this death. Wainewright then invited his wife's mother Mrs Abercromby to come and stay and she brought her two daughters. Mrs Abercromby soon passed away (by way of poison) and Wainewright had insured her daughter Helen for a considerable sum of money. Helen, despite being a healthy young woman, then died suddenly but Wainewright was to be frustrated because the insurance company refused to pay out.

The legend goes that Mrs Abercromby had been bumped off by Wainewright in swift fashion when she began inquiring why an insurance policy had been taken out on her daughter. Wainewright spent five years trying to fight the insurance company for the money for Helen's death but he seemed to admit defeat in the end and, mindful of the fact that his financial activities were attracting unwelcome interest, he fled to France. In France he became close to a woman and then had life insurance taken out on her father. No prizes for guessing what happened next.

Thomas Griffiths Wainewright returned to England £3,000 richer but was arrested for financial fraud as a result of fake signatures on stock shares. Wainewright was found guilty and sent to a penal colony in Australia. Oddly, it was financial fraud rather than murder that saw him in court. Wainewright had had a few spells behind bars during his five year stay in France and was found to have strychnine among his possessions. He was clearly a poisoner who would kill anyone so long as there was money in it for him.

Thomas Griffiths Wainewright died in Tasmania in 1858. He was allowed to paint in Australia and had a certain amount of freedom. It was probably a lot better than being sent to an English prison. Trivia - while Wainewright was in prison awaiting his trial, Charles

Dickens visited the prison and met Thomas Griffiths Wainewright.

WILLIAM PALMER was born in Staffordshire in 1824. He tends to be known as The Rugeley Poisoner or The Prince of Poisoners in true crime articles. One of Palmer's early jobs was as an assistant in a Liverpool chemist but he was fired when he was caught stealing. He later set up an illegal abortion clinic before eventually training as real doctor in London. Palmer returned to Staffordshire to set up a practice. Despite his new medical qualifications, Palmer was not someone you'd want to be your doctor. He had a drink problem and racked up huge gambling debts. He also had a large number of children - many of them illegitimate.

Palmer hit upon a way to keep his creditors at bay. It was a method that numerous murderers have deployed through the centuries. Palmer decided to start bumping off relatives to get the insurance money. Strychnine was his poison of choice. The first person he murdered was his mother in law. She was insured for a tidy sum. Four of Palmer's children then died in sudden and mysterious circumstances though at the time this didn't come under great scrutiny because - sadly - it was not uncommon for infants to die in that era.

What should have been more suspicious was the death of Palmer's wife Ann. She was only 27 when she died and William Palmer had recently taken out insurance on her. The cause of death for Ann was cited as cholera. William Palmer then took out life insurance on his brother Walter and - sure enough - Walter soon kicked the bucket. However, the insurance company refused to pay up because they sensed there was something dodgy about William Palmer. William was in big trouble by now because his debts were crippling him and he was even being blackmailed by a former lover.

In 1855, William Palmer went to watch some horse racing in Shrewsbury with a man named John Parsons Cook. Cook, like Palmer, was addicted to gambling. That day, Cook had a lot more success than Palmer at the races and won a number of sizeable bets. They visited a pub to celebrate but Cook fell ill. Naturally, William Palmer generously offered to go and collect the incapacitated Cook's winnings from the horse racing. No prizes for guessing why Cook had fallen ill.

Not long after this, a fifth child of Palmer died and John Parsons Cook passed away. A maid who sampled some broth Palmer had made for Cook also fell ill. The stepfather of John Parsons Cook was rightly suspicious of all of this and ordered an autopsy to be carried out. It transpired that John Parsons Cook had been poisoned. It didn't take Sherlock Holmes to work out who had poisoned him. It was difficult to establish any evidence in most of the deaths attributed to Palmer but the poisoning of Cook was more than sufficient to seal his fate - and that poisoning was proven beyond doubt.

William Palmer was found guilty at the Old Bailey (the trial was not held in Staffordshire because local feeling was so hostile to Palmer it was felt he wouldn't get a fair trial there) and sentenced to death. William Palmer was hung at Stafford prison on the 14th of June 1856. Thirty thousand people turned up to watch him die. People in those days really did love a good old public execution! Trivia - Charles Dickens (him again!) called Palmer "the greatest villain that ever stood in the Old Bailey."

EDWARD WILLIAM PRITCHARD was born in Hampshire in 1825. He became a doctor and was a surgeon on a Royal Navy ship. On his return to England he met his wife Mary Jane Taylor and eventually settled in Yorkshire for a time. Pritchard was a GP and also wrote books. Edward William Pritchard had a combover and a huge beard. He looked like a character in a Dickens novel. His life seemed pretty good from the outside but he was racking up debts and clearly a troubled man in private.

In 1859, Pritchard moved to Scotland and ended up living in Glasgow. Four years later there was a strange and dramatic incident when a fire broke out at the house Pritchard was living in. One of the servants, a young woman named Elizabeth McGrain, died in the fire. The puzzling thing about the death was that Elizabeth did not apear to have made any attempt to escape from the fire - despite the fact that it would have been possible for her to do so.

In 1885, Pritchard's mother in law Jane Taylor died while being treated by him. Edward William Pritchard had poisoned her. A month later Pritchard's wife died at the age of 38. She had also been poisoned. The local doctor refused to sign the death certificates because he deemed these two deaths in such close proximity to be highly suspicious (to say the least). Pritchard therefore wrote the certificates himself.

The doctor who refused to write the death certificates then wrote to the procurator fiscal (public prosecutor) highlighting his suspicions about Pritchard. Pritchard, who was quite a vain and bombastic man, expressed outrage at having his good name besmirched by these rumours. He was soon put in his place though when his mother in law and wife were exhumed and found to have been killed by the poison antimony. A hearing in Edinburgh, which lasted less than a week, found Edward William Pritchard guilty.

The servant girl dying in the fire now seemed mightily suspicious in hindsight. Do she not try to escape from the fire because she had been drugged or incapacitated? Pritchard is heavily suspected of being involved in this death too. On the 28th of July 1865, Edward William Pritchard was hung in the last public execution carried out in Scotland. 80,000 people turned up to see how go to the gallows. In those days there was nothing people liked more than a good execution.

The trial seemed to suggest that Pritchard had been having an affair with 15-year-old servant Mary MacLeod. It appears then that the motive for murder was to get his wife and mother in law out of the way so he could replace them with Mary. Pritchard did reap a decent financial boost from the death of his mother in law so money was most likely a factor too. The evidence proposed that Pritchard's wife had discovered he was carrying on with the servant girl and this is what made Pritchard resort to murder.

Despite all of this, Pritchard even tried to pin the murders on Mary at one point - although he later retracted this. Pritchard put up a determined performance at his hearing but the exhumations made his case hopeless. At one point he even got his two children to come in and say what a great father he was in the faint hope that this might sway things back in his favour! In the end, after he was found guilty, Pritchard made a full confession. Edward William Pritchard became known as The Human Crocodile in Scotland at the time because of the fake crocodile tears he shed at his hearing for the wife he had so heartlessly murdered.

THOMAS NEILL CREAM was born in Glasgow in 1850. Cream tends to be known as The Lambeth Poisoner in true crime lore. Though born in Scotland, Cream was raised in Canada where he became a doctor. Cream then studied in Scotland and London for a time and then returned to North America. In 1876, Cream married a woman named Flora Brooks but she died a year later. The cause of death was cited as consumption but Cream is believed to have murdered her.

In 1879, a woman named Kate Gardener was found dead near Cream's office. She had been poisoned by chloroform and was pregnant. It just so happened that when he was medical student, Cream did a thesis on chloroform. It was something he knew a lot about. When he became a suspect in this death, Cream fled from Canada to the United States. He opened a medical practice in Chicago and performed illegal abortions on local prostitutes. At least two of these prostitutes died as a consequence of Cream.

In 1881, a woman named Alice Montgomery was found dead near Cream's office. She had been poisoned. Though the case was never solved at the time it seems too much of a coincidence that she died so close to where Cream worked. A few months later a man named Daniel Stott died. The connecting factor in these deaths was strychnine poisoning. Cream had been treating Stott for epilepsy. Thomas Neill Cream seemed to have a grisly scam running where he would procure some medicine from a chemist, kill a patient, and then try and blackmail the chemist by saying he'd been supplied with dodgy medicine.

Cream had conspired to kill Daniel Stott with Stott's wife Julia. Julia was having an affair with Cream and had asked him to kill her husband. He was happy to oblige. In the end though this wicked duo were arrested and Julia agreed to testify against Thomas Neill Cream. Cream was given life in prison but released in 1891. The general theory is that Cream's brother bribed the authorities to get him an early release.

After his release, Cream went to London and set up residence in Lambeth. Cream wasted no time in killing again. He poisoned a teenage prostitute and then tried to exort money from the coroner by writing to say he knew who the killer was. Cream killed another prostitute for similar bribery motivations (in this case Cream accused a doctor named

William Broadbent of the killing and tried to get money from Broadbent in return for silence). In April 1892, Cream poisoned two more prostitutes by lacing Guinness with strychnine.

Thomas Neill Cream was clearly an intelligent and crafty man but it turned out he wasn't nearly as intelligent and crafty as he had assumed. The police had noticed that the blackmail letters mentioned the murder of a prostitute named Matilda Clover. This was odd because the death was put down to natural causes. Cream also made the mistake of giving an American friend a tour of sites in Lambeth where all these strange local deaths had abounded. The friend (who was obviously suspicious of Cream) told Scotland Yard of this and it was clearly of great interest to them.

The police began to observe and follow Cream and they soon saw that he frequently visited and consorted with local prostitutes. Cream was arrested and put on trial in October 1892. He was sentenced to death and hung at Newgate Prison. According to folklore, before he was hung, Cream confessed that he was Jack the

Ripper. This is very disputed though and probably not true. Cream only arrived in London after the last Ripper murders and was actually in prison during some of the Ripper's activities. Those who think Cream is a Ripper suspect argue that he could have been secretly released thanks to his brother's bribes and authority.

The obvious counter argument to the theory that Cream was the Ripper is that he poisoned his victims. He had a very different MO to the more hands-on and bloodthirsty Ripper. The main motivation for Cream's murders was money. There was considerable evidence too though that he enjoyed killing people and became addicted to the sense of power this gave him. It doesn't seem unlikely at all that Cream killed more people than we know of - especially as he seemed to target street prostitutes.

GEORGE CHAPMAN was born Seweryn Antonowicz Klosowski in Poland in 1865. He later changed his name to George Chapman when he moved to England. He took the name after meeting a woman named Annie Chapman (not the Ripper victim - this was a different Annie Chapman). As a young man in Poland, Chapman had some surgical training but he couldn't qualify as a doctor in England and became a hairdresser instead. In October 1889 he married Lucy Baderski and had a shop off Whitechapel High Street. Chapman moved to America for a time but then moved back to England and took up with a woman named Isabella Spink to run a public house.

It seems that Chapman would have endless mistresses and pretend they were his wives (it obviously wasn't respectable in those days to live with someone you were not married to). Isabella Spink died at the end of 1897 after falling ill. The symptoms of her illness were severe stomach pains. After Spink's death, Chapman took up with a barmaid named Bessie Taylor but she died at the start of 1901 after developing identical symptoms to those of the late Isabella Spink. Chapman wasted no time in wooing another barmaid - this time the unfortunate Maud Marsh. Maud died at the start of 1902 after suddenly falling ill with - you guessed it - severe stomach pains.

Maud Marsh's mother was highly suspicious of her daughter's sudden death and kicked up such a fuss that the doctor had to order an examination of the body should take place. This post-mortem revealed antimony poisoning. The bodies of the two previous victims were dug up and also found to have been poisoned. George Chapman was put on trial at the Old Bailey and swiftly found guilty of a triple murder. The trial established that Chapman had purchased poison in the past from a chemist and had got £500 from the death of Isabella Spink.

The weird thing was though that Chapman didn't reap any financial windfall for the deaths of his other victims. It therefore remains a slight puzzle establishing motive - although Chapman was clearly a serial fraudster in his life. He once burnt down a pub for the insurance. It is sometimes said that another barmaid he was in a relationship with, one Elizabeth Taylor, was another victim because she also died while she was with Chapman. However, there was no sign of poisoning in Taylor's death and it genuinely appeared to be of natural causes (or an intestinal obstruction in this case).

Chapman was hanged at Wandsworth Prison on April the 7th 1902. That's not quite the end of the story though because George Chapman is an enduring Jack the Ripper suspect. It is said that, in response to media speculation at the time of Chapman's arrest, that Inspector Abberline considered Chapman to be a very plausible Ripper suspect. The main reasons for this are that Chapman had some surgical training and was familiar with Whitechapel. It was also the case that the Ripper murders ceased when Chapman went to live in the United States for a time.

The police investigated Chapman as a Ripper suspect after his death and learned from his original wife Lucy that he used to go out a lot late at night. Chapman was also revealed to have been a violent man who once tried to strangle Lucy and kept a knife under his bed. While all the speculation concerning Chapman and Jack the Ripper is interesting and at times quite convincing the one big flaw in the theory that he was the Ripper comes with the disparity in the method of murders. The Ripper killed his victims in gruesome fashion and then mutilated the bodies. Chapman on the other hand was a poisoner and never mutilated any of his victims.

Why would Jack the Ripper resort to poison? And if Chapman was Jack the Ripper why was he killing barmaids (and attracting suspicion) when he could just as easily go out and kill a prostitute? Another reason why some are not convinced by the theory that Chapman was Jack the Ripper is that they don't believe there is any evidence that the Ripper had any medical training. They would argue that Chapman, who trained as a surgeon in Poland, would have shown much more skill than the Ripper did in cutting up the victims.

WALTER HORSEFORD was a Cambridgeshire farmer who was hung for poisoning Annie Holmes in 1887. Horsford was 26 at the time. Annie was his cousin but also his lover. She was a widow with children. It is believed that Horseford poisoned her with strychnine after she told him she was pregnant. Walter Horseford, like many killers, was a dodgy character from a young age. He was a grocer as a very young man but lost his position for theft and embezzlement. He landed on his feet as a farmer though and was good at this profession.

Horseford was rumbled quite soon for the murder of Annie Holmes. The police found a large quantity of strychnine in his possession. He had sent the poison to Annie pretending it was medicine. His instructions were to take it with a little water - and this is exactly what Annie did. Horseford promised Annie the medicine was harmless but he knew full well it would kill her. Horseford was executed at Cambridge prison in June 1897 for Annie's murder. However, this is not the end of the story. There seems to be considerable evidence that Horseford killed at least three other people.

His former fiancée Fanny James died in 1890. Just like Annie Holmes, Fanny died soon after telling Walter Horseford she was pregnant. Those around Fanny said that her sudden demise was consistent with someone who had been poisoned. The official cause of death, believe it or not, was put down to Fanny eating a large supper! I'm no medical expert but I've never heard of anyone dropping dead because they ate a big dinner! Another suspicious case involving Horseford was a relative of Fanny James who died suddenly after drinking some beer Horseford had supplied for him.

The victim was a farm worker who had just spent the day threshing wheat. It seems more than a coincidence that this healthy man expired after drinking something given to him by Horseford. What the motive was in this death remains unclear but Horseford clearly wanted this chap out of the way. A fourth murder commonly attributed to Horserford is that of an unknown woman from Peterborough who he was having an affair with. This young woman is said to have died after receiving a parcel from Horseford. That would match the MO of this killer and be fairly identical to the death of Annie Holmes. Walter Horseford was a very cold and cunning man. Who knows how many people he might really have murdered?

ROBERT GEORGE CLEMENTS was born in Belfast in 1880. You might say that he was sort of like the male version of one of those female Black Widow killers. Clements was a doctor and a fellow of the Royal College of Surgeons. He was married four times and all of his wives died in rather suspicious circumstances. The fact that his wives tended to be rich with inherited wealth merely added to the strong suspicion that Clements was marrying wealthy women and bumping them off to get his hands on the money. Edith Annie Mercier, the first wife of Clements, died of what was called sleeping sickness. Edith was the daughter of a wealthy mill owner and was only 40 when she died.

Mary McCreary, the second wife of Clements, died suddenly at the age of 25 in 1925. The cause of death was cited as endocarditis. Mary was the daughter of a wealthy industrialist. One would imagine that, as a doctor himself, Clements was able to conjure convincing medical theories of his own when his wives died and so managed to deflect undue suspicion. In 1939, Clements lost a third wife when Sarah Kathleen Burke died. Her death was also ascribed to endocarditis. The body was cremated in rapid fashion - which was obviously rather suspicious.

The last wife of Robert George Clements was Amy Victoria Barnett. Amy was the daughter of a wealthy man named Reginald W. G. Barnett - who was one of Clements' patients. Amy died in 1947, officially as a result of myeloid leukemia. The death of wife number four led to Robert George Clements coming under a lot of suspicion. To have one wife die in that era was nothing unusual but four seemed a trifle out of the ordinary. Not only had all four of his wives died but Robert George Clements had written the death certificates himself. You could say that he was almost too obvious in his crimes. He was bound to attract suspicion sooner or later.

Three of his wives were very wealthy when he married them but by the time of their deaths Robert George Clements had managed to fritter away most of their fortunes. One can see how a fairly convincing criminal case against Clements could be constructed. He appeared to marry wealthy women and then - when he sensed the money was running out - he bumped them off and looked for a new wife. The hasty cremation was also very suspicious. The police decided in the end there was more than enough evidence to suggest that Clements had murdered his wives but when they went to speak to him he had already committed suicide with morphine.

Robert George Clements had clearly realised the game was up and decided to end it all before he was dragged into a police cell and court. An autopsy was then conducted on Amy Victoria Barnett and the conclusion was that she'd been poisoned with morphine - thus seeming to confirm that Robert George Clements really had been killing his wives. There was a sad coda to this case because the doctor who had performed the first autopsy on Amy committed suicide in shame after the second autopsy confirmed he had not deduced that Amy had died of morphine poisoning. As for the late Robert George Clements, well, the evidence that he was serial murderer of wives was now sadly established. Clements had simply decided to skip the trial and likely execution and do away with himself.

RONALD CLARK O'BRYAN was born in Houston in 1944. O'Bryan sometimes worked as an optician and was also a deacon at the local church. A fine pillar of the community you might say. Well, if you did say that you would be completely wrong I'm afraid. In reality, O'Bryan was often unemployed and seemed to have difficulty holding down a job. He had racked up considerable debts which amounted to hundreds of thousands of dollars. O'Bryan was an unhappy man crippled by these debts. His mental health was eroding fast. He decided he had to take drastic action to resolve this problem. As a solution to his financial woes, O'Bryan came up with a plan which was so heartless and evil it defied comprehension.

On Halloween night in 1974, O'Bryan took his two kids out trick or treating. He had taken six Pixy Stix (a sweet and sour colored powdered candy usually packaged in a wrapper that resembles a drinking straw) and laced them with potassium cyanide. Ronald Clark O'Bryan gave one of these poisoned candies to his eight year-son Timothy because he wanted the insurance money from his son's death. This was beyond evil. What sort of person would give their child poisoned food?

Timothy went into convulsions and died. That wasn't even the half of it. O'Bryan also gave poisoned candy to his young daughter and several other children but - mercifully - none of them ate the candy. One child tried to eat the candy but couldn't get the wrapper off and gave up. The wrapper saved that boy's life. Ronald Clark O'Bryan was not a suspect at first but the police soon began to zero in on him. It transpired that he had only taken his children to a couple of nearby streets trick or treating. They hadn't gone far at all. That was deemed suspicious. O'Bryan's plan was obviously to make it seem as if Timothy had got the poisoned candy from one of the houses they knocked on.

The police wanted to know which house had handed out the poisoned Pixy Stix to the kids but the house O'Bryan named belonged to an air traffic controller who wasn't even at home on Halloween night. Upon further investigation the police found out that O'Bryan was heavily in debt and had recently taken out life insurance policies on his two children. They also found out he had recently been seen in a chemical store in Houston. The police believe that O'Bryan's plan was to kill his two children for the insurance but also poison other random kids in the area (by handing out the Pixy Stix) to make it look like someone had randomly handed out poisoned candy. This ruse obviously didn't work.

The jury didn't take very long to find O'Bryan guilty - despite his weak attempts to pretend he was innocent. It transpired during the trial that O'Brien had researched cyanide before Halloween and during his son's funeral had talked about going on a nice holiday with the insurance money. He was a truly despicable man. Ronald Clark O'Bryan was sentenced to death by electric chair. This happened in 1984. For his last meal on death row he had steak and fries followed by Boston cream pie. A group outside the prison yelled 'Trick or Treat!' and threw candy at anti-capital punishment protesters as this dreadful man was executed. Ronald Clark O'Bryan is inevitably known as the Candyman in true crime. After his conviction his wife got married to someone else. The only happy note to this dreadful case is that the daughter Elizabeth survived because she never got around to eating the Pixy Stix on that tragic Halloween night.

GRAHAM YOUNG was born in Neasden in Middlesex on the 7th of September 1947. As a youth he became obsessed with poisons and chemicals and decided to conduct some experiments of his own. The unwitting guinea pigs in these experiments were his own family! Young's usual method was to lace drinks like tea with thallium and antimony. Thallium can affect your nervous system, lung, heart, liver, and kidney if large amounts are eaten or drunk for short periods of time. Temporary hair loss, vomiting, and diarrhoea can also occur and death may result after exposure to large amounts of thallium for short periods.

Young, now about 14 years-old, began poisoning his stepmother, father, and sister in 1961. He managed to obtain potentially dangerous chemicals from a chemist by pretending to be older than he actually was. Soon, everyone around Graham Young seemed to be suffering from dreadful stomach pains - even including some pupils at his school.

The family began to have suspicions about Graham Young but they couldn't find any firm evidence and he naturally denied everything (Young actually blamed his sister). When his mother died it was put down to a medical complaint. Graham (of course) took the chance to slip some poison into food at his mother's funeral. By now, suspicions about Graham Young and his activities were spreading beyond the family.

One of his teachers (who found poisonous chemicals in Young's desk) suspected he was up to something dangerous. The police became involved and Young was found to have thallium and antimony in his possession. He confessed to secretly administering poison to his family and a school friend. Young was sent to Broadmoor Hospital - where he was the youngest inmate for many years. He was charged with killing his stepmother.

Graham Young spent nine years at Broadmoor. It is alleged that he may even have killed someone at Broadmoor by extracting poison from laurel bush leaves in the gardens. When he was released from Broadmoor in 1971, Young soon went back to his old ways. He somehow managed to purchase antimony potassium tartrate and thalium from a chemist. While attending a storekeeping course in Slough, Young poisoned a man named Trevor Sparkes more than once. Sparkes did not die but he was violently ill from his ordeal.

Graham Young then secured a job at John Hadland Laboratories in Bovingdon, Hertfordshire. Broadmoor provided him with a reference but - amazingly - did not inform John Hadland Laboratories that Young was a convicted poisoner! One of Young's duties at the lab was to push the tea trolley around. Talk about a recipe for disaster! You can probably guess what happened next.

Very soon a mysterious 'bug' at the lab had everyone coming down with dreadful stomach pains.

It was later established that Young would actually poison people as a way of gaining promotion. Bob Egle died as a result of poisoning and Ron Hewitt left the firm after falling ill. As a consequence of this respective death and departure, Graham Young was promoted to head storeroom clerk. Young would keep diaries of his activities and keep abreast of how his various poisonings were affecting the victims. If anyone was rude to him he would give them a dose of poison and then note how much he was enjoying their discomfort. Young next poisoned two men named David Tilson and Jethro Batt with thalium. They both survived but suffered dreadfully. Their hair fell out and they were bedridden and deeply ill.

Fred Biggs, a 56-year-old local councillor, was the next victim. Biggs worked part time at the lab and had his tea poisoned by Young. He died as a result of the poisoning. Biggs was poisoned so badly that his skin started to peel away. By now the staff at John Hadland Laboratories had become very suspicious of Graham Young. They had deduced two very salient things. The first was that this violent and mysterious stomach bug had only began swirling around when Graham Young joined the firm. The second thing they deduced was that Graham Young never seemed to be affected! That was more than a little suspicious.

The police did a (long overdue) check on Graham Young and found out about his storied history as a prolific poisoner. They searched his home and found that he had a very large stash of poisons. They also found his diaries in which he'd written copious notes about who he had poisoned and what effects the chemicals had on them. Graham Young knew the game was up now and confessed. He even confessed to murdering his late stepmother. Graham Young was highly intelligent but deeply disturbed. The police found that his room was full of swastikas and pictures of Adolf Hitler.

Young was charged with two counts of murder, two counts of attempted murder, four counts of administering poison with intent to injure and four counts of administering poison with intent to cause grievous bodily harm. He (rather preposterously) pleaded not guilty and tried to claim that his diary was not real but simply a fantasy novel he was writing. This defence was predictably hopeless and he was sentenced to life in prison. Young is generally credited with at least three murders but poisoned about 80+ people. Who knows how many people he might have killed if he'd stayed in society for a few years longer.

It is said that in prison Young became a friend of the Moors Murderer Ian Brady. Graham Young died in prison in 1990 at the age of 42. The cause of death was a heart attack. A brilliant 1995 film called The Young Poisoner's Handbook was loosely based on Graham Young. * The version of Young depicted in the film though is more likeable than the real person. In 2005, a Japanese schoolgirl was arrested for poisoning her mother with thallium. She had become obsessed with the story of Graham Young after watching The Young Poisoner's Handbook.

CHARLES ALBANESE was born in Chicago in 1947. He was something of an idle young man but had a stint as a car salesman. Albanese desired most of all to make lots of money without having to work too hard for that money. Join the club Charlie! In that he was a lot like the rest of us. The difference being that Charlie was fully prepared to kill for that money. Most of us want to be rich but we draw the line at actually harming anyone to achieve this. That's the key difference between killers and ordinary people. Killers have a lump of coal where their heart is supposed to be. You could accurately describe Albanese as a financially motivated killer. Radford University's research suggested that 31% of killers murder for financial reasons.

Albanese was another in the long line of true crime poisoners. True crime history is positively (if you'll pardon the pun) laced with murderous poisoners. The victims of Albanese were all relatives of either him or his wife. He killed his wife's mother and grandmother with arsenic in an attempt to shift the family inheritance down a few generations. Charlie would often visit these relatives in a retirement community and bring them gifts and food. They probably thought he was a really nice man. Little did they know he planned to poison them. He was successful in this too and soon had his mother and grandmother in law shuffling off this mortal coil by way of arsenic laced grub.

Charlie's wife (who wasn't part of the poisoning scheme and had no idea her her husband was a murderous criminal) was awarded $150,000 as a result of these murders. The weird thing by this point is that Charlie's father had a Die Casting company and Charles Albanese worked there and earned a decent salary. It isn't as if Charlie was destitute or starved of money. He had a pretty decent standard of living working for his father. Most people would have been perfectly content with the money he earned. It was pure greed which made him also murder relatives for the inheritance. Charlie always wanted more money. They say money is the root of all evil and that was certainly the case with Charles Albanese.

In 1980, the same year as his previous murders, Albanese had a falling out with his father and was demoted in the family company. Charlie seemed to take this demotion surprisingly well though and even began bringing his father cookies as a gift whenever he saw him. No prizes for guessing what was in these biscuits. Charlie's father was poisoned to death by cookies and as a consequence Charles Albanese inherited $250,000 and complete control over the family business. Charlie now had everything he had ever desired. He was awash with money and the family business was his and his alone. What could possibly go wrong? Well, just about everything as it turned out.

The trouble began for Charlie when the McHenry County Coroner, Alvin Querhammer, found arsenic in the body of Charlie's father and so a criminal investigation was launched. The bodies of the two other recently deceased relatives were examined and also found to contain arsenic. The police then discovered that Charles Albanese had been sold some arsenic. The game was nearly up for Charlie. A noose of damning evidence was being drawn ever tighter around his neck.

At this time, Charlie was set to go away with his wife and mother on a trip. The police strongly suspected that Charlie planned to poison his mother on this trip for the last of the family inheritance money. Given what he'd already done, Charles Albanese was probably more than capable of killing his dear old mother. If he had killed his mother then - in terms of statistics - this would have put Albanese in serial killer territory. When the police saw how much money Charles Albanese and his wife had made from the deaths of the three deceased relatives it became rather obvious that he must have been the killer. The evidence against him was overwhelming.

Charles Albanese was tried in two separate jurisdictions and executed via lethal injection at the Stateville Correctional Center in 1995 (as true crime buffs will be well aware, once someone is sentenced to death in the United States it can take years and decades before the execution actually takes place). Albanese never expressed any remorse for his crimes and displayed no emotion in court. He was simply a very cold and ruthless man.

* The Young Poisoner's Handbook is a great little forgotten British film from 1995 directed by Benjamin Ross. The film revolves around Graham Young (Hugh O'Conor), a high IQ misfit and introverted outsider who develops a remarkable scientific ability and fascination from a very young age. The story begins in 1961 with Graham 14-years-old and living a fairly dull life in the drab working class suburbia of Neasden with his dysfunctional television obsessed parents (played Ruth Sheen and Roger Lloyd Pack) and very annoying older sister Winnie (the late Charlotte Coleman). Graham, who has a very strange sense of himself and the world, is vaguely repulsed by his parents and the vain Winnie and spends most of his time in his bedroom conducting elaborate chemistry experiments in the hope of somehow creating a diamond. After putting antimony sulfide in his vials he inadvertently produces a lethal toxin which he soon becomes obsessed by. Rapidly discovering new things about the world of toxins all the time, Graham dreams about becoming the most brilliant poisoner of all time and decides the first test case will be

his awful stepmother...

The Young Poisoner's Handbook is loosely based on the story of the real life Graham Young who became known as the 'Teacup Poisoner' for his somewhat anti-social activities in the sixties and early seventies. The real Young though was a more prosaic character, just a plain nutcase and obsessed with Nazis. The Graham Young in this film is, understandably for cinematic purposes, very different and brilliantly played by Hugh O'Conor. O'Conor's Graham Young is a genius, outwardly courteous, gentle and well spoken (with a very dry sense of humour) and strangely rather likeable. The only problem is that the coldly calculating Graham, with his wide-eyed scientific curiosity, has no heart or emotions whatsoever and is far more concerned with his ongoing chemical experiments than the welfare of individual human beings. "Life is a series of illusions that only a scientist could strip away," reflects Graham with his clinical view of everything.

It is only when Graham tries to poison his father that he is caught and sent to Harshhurst Hospital, an institution for the criminally insane. Oddly, Graham wants to be caught for the notoriety and fame, a crucial thing for the curriculum vitae of any great poisoner in his own estimation. Deemed fit to re-enter society several years later by the liberal and trendy dream analysing prison psychiatrist Dr Zeigler (Anthony Sher), Graham is fixed up with a menial job as a storekeeper at a small, cheerful, photographic laboratory. The question of how long will he be able to resist his scientific fascination with poisoning people makes for a compelling final arc to the film, especially as Graham is now placed in an environment full of opportunity and temptation with an abundance of both chemicals and people.

Despite the macabre nature of the story, The Young Poisoner's Handbook is not a horror film or a thriller. It's more of an offbeat black comedy and social satire with a sneakily malevolent wit, sort of like a cross between A Clockwork Orange and a vintage Ealing comedy. The story is certainly morbidly compelling though from very early on when Graham poisons his stepmother and keeps a meticulous scientific diary charting her progress as he experiments and tinkers with the dosage. This is probably the darkest portion of the film but The Young Poisoner's Handbook always offsets its subject matter with a very genteel British atmosphere and a sly sense of humour. Plus, his stepmother is so unpleasant your sympathy leans towards Graham here - "You contaminate everything you touch. I'm going to scrub you till you are raw!"

Although The Young Poisoner's Handbook is set in a very down to earth English suburbia, it maintains a slightly heightened reality and an offbeat quality that lifts it well above the numerous abysmal British films made on the back on Lottery money from the nineties onwards. This is a film that deserved a much wider audience and following. The Young Poisoner's Handbook also paints an effectively dull portrait of ordinary sixties working class life and interestingly conveys the gradual social shifts of the time as it moves into the somewhat more kitsch seventies. The film is essentially three acts, consisting of Graham's early experiments with his family, his time in prison and then his release. The prison section is possibly the only part of the film that might slightly sag or seem a trifle familiar to some viewers although it's always absorbing as Graham befriends the pioneering psychiatrist Zeigler and persuades the authorities that he is now completely sane and cured. The Young Poisoner's Handbook seems to be critical in particular of trendy psychiatrists playing God and deciding when some sociopath or murderer is suitable to be released back into society.

Having Graham lumbered with a job in brown overalls for which he is, of course, ridiculously too intelligent, provides some funny little moments and The Young Poisoner's Handbook does a great job in capturing the sometimes lairy and often tedious banter of a small factory type environment where everybody thinks they are a comedian. The misanthropic Graham's attempts to fit into his new job without standing out too much make for compelling viewing and the third act really amps up the tension as Graham goes about his dull job, which includes serving everybody a mug of tea! There is a great little moment where Graham is waiting to be interviewed for the job and sighs heavily when a youngster next to him complains that the job will be impossible to get because the employer wants O'Levels, as if that was some preposterously out of reach qualification that no mere mortal could ever aspire to. There is also another amusing moment when Graham starts questioning a police scientific expert and proves considerably more knowledgeable, much to the bewilderment of the older man. O'Conor gives a very compelling and impressive performance as Graham and his emotionless and analytical narration throughout the film is spot-on. The Young Poisoner's Handbook will probably not appeal to everyone, but this is a dark, amusing and very entertaining film that deserves more of a cult following.

CHAPTER TWO - SHE SEEMED LIKE SUCH A NICE OLD LADY

Some of the most famous poisoners were grandmothers or what appeared to nice old ladies. What you might call wolves in sheep's clothing. Poison is a popular method of murder for older women in true crime history because it doesn't require brute force or a weapon of any kind. You can simply slip it in a cake or some tea. Anything you want. A lot of poisoners think they stand a much better chance of getting away with their crime through poisoning but this is obviously a misguided view. It might be more complex to capture a poisoner than a mad axeman but the police tend to catch up with poisoners in the end. In this chapter we'll take a look at some deadly poisoners who seemed - on the surface - to be nice old ladies and so were able to go about their wicked deeds in plain sight.

BABA ANUJKA was born in Romania in 1838. She tends to be known as The Witch of Vladimirovac in true crime lore. As a young woman, Anujka had an affair with an army officer but he abandoned her. Not only that but he gave her an STD too. This experience is said to have left her with a hatred of men. She did though later get married and have eleven children. Tragedy struck multiple times though and only one of the children actually survived childhood.

Baba Anujka eventually became interested in herbalism and came up with an idea for a way to make money. She made her own 'love potions' which she sold to women who had unhappy marriages. Baba Anujka told the women that if they gave their husbands these potions the husband would become madly in love with them again and never be unfaithful. The love potions were marketed as 'magic water'. As this was an age where quack doctors flourished, Baba Anujka did a roaring trade in these bogus love potions and soon had many female customers eager to try them on their wayward and disinterested husbands.

There was only one problem though. The love potions, unknown to the women, were festooned with arsenic and toxins. Baba Anujka was not really interested in saving marriages. She was more interested in killing men. How many men died as a result of Baba Anujka's love potions? The true figure is impossible to verify but some estimates place the victim count at 150. At the very least it is believed that Baba Anujka killed fifty men with her deadly home brewed potions. Her murderous ruse came to an end when a woman named Stana Momirov had relatives die as a result of the potions and was arrested on suspicion of poisoning. Momirov told the authorities that she had got the potions from Baba Anujka.

Anujka was actually acquitted at her first trial in 1915 but she was later arrested again in 1928 when more evidence against her came to light. She was around 90 years-old when she was arrested - which must surely make her a strong contender for the oldest serial killer at the time of capture. Baba Anujka was sentenced to fifteen years in prison at her second trial. The lightish sentence was probably a consequence of the fact that they only had enough evidence to pin two murders on her. She was released on medical grounds eight years later and died in 1938 at the ripe old age of 100. This little old lady didn't look like much of a threat to anyone but purely in statistical terms she was one of the most prolific serial killers of all time.

SARAH JANE ROBINSON was born in Ireland in 1838. When she was in her early teens her family moved to the United States. She married a man named Moses Robinson in 1858 and they lived in Sherborn, Massachusetts. Robinson is said to have met a man named Thomas R. Smith at the local church though and Smith became something of an accomplice in the awful crimes that followed. From 1881 onwards, members of the Robinson family began to fall ill with agonising stomach pains. It was naturally (and suspiciously) Sarah Jane Robinson who cared for these ill relatives. She was the one in charge of the medicine cabinet.

Nearly all of the ill (and soon to expire) relatives had life insurance through The Order of Pilgrim Fathers. The Order of Pilgrim Fathers was a local social group which offered affordable insurance to those who weren't wealthy. Sarah Jane took full advantage of this affordable insurance scheme in the deadliest way possible. Money was the primary motivation for her murders. She even poisoned the family's landlord and then tried to charge his family a fee for her 'nursing' services! She is alleged to have also stolen money from him.

As you might imagine, with all these relatives popping their clogs and the life insurance all going to Sarah Jane, it was only a matter of time before suspicion began to rear its head. Robinson was incredibly ruthless. She even killed her daughter and a seven year-old nephew. Sarah Jane was caught when her son William died but seemed to blame his mother for his illness before he passed away. The accusations of William were enough for a doctor to have tests done on his stomach tissue at a university after he died. This test established that William had been killed by arsenic poisoning.

Sarah Jane and two alleged accomplices (including of course Thomas R. Smith) were arrested. Further exhumations and tests confirmed that numerous Robinson family members (and their landlord to boot) had been poisoned. Sarah Jane pretended to be insane at first in an effort to dodge a trial and serious charges but this ruse was quickly seen through. She was originally sentenced to death but this was then commuted to life in prison. A year after the case a family who had moved into the old Robinson family home found a big box of rat poison hidden up the fireplace. Sarah Jane's guilt was never in question. She died in prison in 1906 at the age of 67. Robinson would become known as The Boston Borgia for her crimes.

LEONARDA CIANCIULLI was born in Montella, Avellino, in 1894. Leonarda Cianciulli was a serial killer active in Italy during World War 2. Her murders were unusual because they were motivated by a belief in black magic. Cianciulli believed that if she offered up some human sacrifices this would prevent her soldier son from coming to any harm in the war. She subsequently killed three women because of these delusions. The story of Leonarda Cianciulli was given a macabre gloss by what she did to her victims after she killed them. She used the blood from her victims in a recipe for tea cakes. Cianciulli also turned her last victim into bars of soap. And yes, Leonarda Cianciulli is said to have sampled the cakes she made from her unfortunate victims.

Her first victim was a spinster named Faustina Sett who had come to Cianciulli for advice in matters of the heart. She wanted Cianciulli to help her find a husband. Cianciulli told Sett she knew of a man but Sett would have to travel to meet him. Cianciulli told Sett to write postcards and post them when she got there. She then drugged Sett with tainted wine and chopped the body up, keeping the blood in a basin. Cianciulli then made cakes out of the blood.

Of her victim blood cakes, Leonarda Cianciulli said - "I threw the pieces into a pot, added seven kilos of caustic soda, which I had bought to make soap, and stirred the mixture until the pieces dissolved in a thick, dark mush that I poured into several buckets and emptied in a nearby septic tank. As for the blood in the basin, I waited until it had coagulated, dried it in the oven, ground it and mixed it with flour, sugar, chocolate, milk and eggs, as well as a bit of margarine, kneading all the ingredients together. I made lots of crunchy tea cakes and served them to the ladies who came to visit, though Giuseppe and I also ate them."

Cianciulli's next victim was Francesca Soav, a woman who required help finding a job. Cianciulli said she had found a suitable position somewhere but then - as before - drugged the victim and made cakes from the dead body after boiling down the other remains. Although these sacrifices were supposed to be some sort of 'dark magic' offerings for the safety of her son, money was an equal motivation. Cianciulli had obtained money from both victims for her services.

The last victim was Virginia Cacioppo. Virginia Cacioppo was a soprano who Cianciulli claimed to have found a secretarial position for. This victim was not just made into cakes but also soap. "She ended up in the pot, like the other two...her flesh was fat and white, when it had melted I added a bottle of cologne, and after a long time on the boil I was able to make some most acceptable creamy soap. I gave bars to neighbours and acquaintances. The cakes, too, were better: that woman was really sweet." Cianciulli said she almost decapitated Virginia Cacioppo by striking her with an axe.

Cianciulli was given a long prison sentence and died in a criminal asylum in 1970. She was 76 years-old. Cianciulli had a troubled time as a young woman as her parents didn't approve of her marriage. She also lost several to her children to miscarriages or illness. This sad experience left her a very superstitious woman who believed in fortune tellers and the occult. This strong belief in the occult is the only real explanation one can put forward as a reason for her bizarre crimes.

NANNIE DOSS was born in Blue Mountain, Alabama, in 1905. Here is one of the most unlikely serial killers. Nannie Doss was a benign looking grandmother who killed eleven relatives before her crimes were uncovered. She is forever known in true crime circles as The Giggling Granny. She showed no remorse at her crimes and even seemed amused whenever she had to reflect on them. The story of Nannie Doss began with her working on a farm as a child. This wasn't much of a life and she hated it. She wasn't in school much thanks to her farm duties and so was never the most intelligent person in the world. She got married at sixteen and had four children - two of whom died. This first marriage didn't last long. Nannie's husband seemed to despise her and was never at home. She was said to drink a lot to curb her loneliness.

Her second marriage was more enduring. Doss spent sixteen years with her second husband and gained some grandchildren over this period. However, two of these grandchildren died while in the custody of Nannie Doss. This same year, Nannie's husband also died. The culprit in these suspicious deaths was Nannie Doss. Nannie's daughter was very suspicious of her mother because she noticed that Nannie had a bizarre habit of sticking pins in the grandchildren when no one was looking. Nannie's husband was a victim of rat poison. Nannie would usually put the poison in cakes she had baked and then serve it up to the victim - in this case her husband. However, the authorities treated none of these deaths as suspicious.

The deadly deeds of Nannie Doss were not over yet. She married for a third time but her new husband didn't last very long. He was presumed to have died of a heart attack but that doesn't seem very likely with Nannie Doss around. Nannie then burnt their house down so that she would be entitled to insurance money. Nannie married again and quickly dispatched her latest husband with rat poison. She then murdered her mother.

In 1953, Nannie found another husband and poisoned him to get her hands on the life insurance polices in his name. This time though her luck finally ran out. When the authorities (not before time you might suggest!) became suspicious of yet another death connected to Nannie Doss, a medical examination found huge amounts of arsenic in the body of her latest (late) husband. Nannie Doss was arrested and confessed to all the murders. She giggled when she made her confession and seemed completely relaxed and calm talking about her crimes. Nannie Doss seemed to actually enjoy talking about the murders she had committed and acted as if it had all been great fun.

The only possible explanation for Nannie Doss is that as a child she apparently suffered a bad head injury when she was hit with a metal bar (that came off a train). It seems plausible that this left her with some sort of mental impairment. She was clearly not a sane or normal woman. A surprisingly high number of serial killers received head injuries from an accident when still a child. There is a theory that this impairs the part of the brain responsible for ruminating on the consequences of one's actions.

Nannie Doss was sentenced to life in prison at her trial. Her gender is probably the only thing that saved her from the death penalty. She died in the Oklahoma State Penitentiary in 1965 at the age of 59. It is said that her last husband was found with enough arsenic in him to kill a horse. Nannie Doss liked to put arsenic in cakes but she also laced moonshine with poison and gave it to her husbands. When she was in custody she denied that her motivation for the murders had been financial. Nannie Doss said she was simply looking for the perfect husband. "I was searching for the perfect mate," she said, by way of explanation for why she kept bumping of husbands. "The real romance of life."

CAROLINE GRILLS was born in Balmain, New South Wales, Australia in 1888. Killers come in all shapes and sizes and Grills is a classic case in point. You might suggest that she was rather like Australia's own version of Nannie Doss. To the outside world, Grills seemed like a perfectly normal and respectable woman. She married in 1908 and had four sons.

Decades later in 1947, Grills became a suspect in the deaths of her 87-year-old stepmother Christine Mickelson; relatives by marriage Angelina Thomas and John Lundberg; and sister in law Mary Anne Mickelson.

The motivation for the murders was presumed to have been financial. Mary Anne Mickelson, for example, had inherited a house from Caroline's father and Caroline obviously presumed that she would be given the house if anything happened to Mary Anne. Grills was a poisoner who used thalium to kill her victims. Thalium, which is odourless and tasteless, used to be widely used a rat poison and was very easy to purchase in stores. Thalium is sometimes called the 'poisoner's poison'.

Caroline Grills would put the thalium in cakes and biscuits she had baked for relatives. One of her other ruses was to slip the poison into a cup of tea she had made for someone. Although the official tally of deaths credited to Grills is four it was established without too much doubt that she also attempted to poison at least three other people. Killers who use poison as a form of murder sometimes tend to become overconfident. They tend to think they have devised a clever and undetectable method of murder but all famous poisoners, just like serial killers who uses guns, knives, or their bare hands, usually get captured in the end.

According to Australia's Dark Heart - 'Throughout 1951-1942 various family members became ill, including Mrs Lundberg, although they suffered with this illness, they all survived. John Downey was one of those whom became ill. He had read a story in a newspaper in October of 1952 about poisonings; this raised his suspicions about 'Aunt Carrie'. He spied her reaching into her apron pocket and then drop something into the cup of tea she was carrying. He had the smarts about him to switch the cups and take a sample of the tea to police. Police tested the sample and found that it contained thallium. This was enough for investigators to examine the deaths of the other members of Grills' family.'

Grills was 63 years-old when she was charged with murder. Bodies were exhumed in this case to establish the guilt of Caroline Grills. A jury took less than twenty minutes to find her guilty. She was initially given a death sentence but this was later relegated to life in prison. Grills became known as Aunt Thally (clever!) in prison. As a consequence of the case, the sale of thalium or products containing thalium was banned in Australia.

Caroline Grills was a rather bewildering presence during the trial and her motivations were never firmly established in any one direction. The prosecutor Mick Rooney QC thought that Grills simply enjoyed killing. He called her "a killer who poisoned for sport, for fun, for the kicks she got out of it, for the hell of it, for the thrill that she and she alone in the world knew the cause of the victims' suffering." Caroline Grills died in 1960 at the age of 71. She was an inmate of Sydney's Long Bay Prison.

MARY ELIZABETH WILSON was born Mary Elizabeth Cassidy in 1889 in Catchgate, Stanley, County Durham. In true crime circles she is known as The Merry Widow of Windy Nook for murdering her husbands. Mary Elizabeth Wilson was a most unlikely serial killer in appearance. She looked like your average run of the mill granny. Her first marriage was in 1914 to a man named John Knowles. The lived in a place called Windy Nook - hence her nickname. Knowles died in 1955 and Mary married again - this time to John Russell. However, Russell died less than two years into the marriage. Mary Elizabeth Wilson had naturally picked up a modest little financial windfall from the death of two husbands in the space of only a couple of years.

In 1957, Mary entered her third marriage when she got hitched to a retired man named Oliver Leonard. This marriage lasted all of twelve days before Oliver Leonard suddenly died. Husband number four was a 76 year-old man named Ernest Wilson. Ernest Wilson was dead within a year of marrying Mary Elizabeth Wilson and Mary happily inherited his house and money. Now, you might think that all these husbands suddenly dropping dead would have attracted more suspicion but apparently the cause of death in each case was cited as natural causes. The medical authorities certainly didn't seem to suspect anything.

The downfall of Mary Elizabeth Wilson was her gallows sense of humour. You might say that Mary rather shot herself in the foot with her own morbid wit. What activated suspicion in her were the jokes she dispensed after these family tragedies. When her third husband died, Mary joked that the sandwiches at the funeral should be saved for the next one. After Ernest Wilson died, Mary is said to have joked to the undertaker that she should get a discount for giving him so much business! This led to much local tittle tattle and innuendo about Mary and the police got involved and eventually exhumed the bodies of two of her husbands. The bodies were found to contain phosphorus. It seems they had been killed by large doses of insect poison.

The day of the planned exhumations, Mary seemed unphased and told the local newspaper - "I am not worried about what they are saying. I can go to the blessed sacrament - I am a Catholic - tomorrow. I take no notice of the tittle-rattle. It is all jealousy. I am not worried at all about what is going on." Despite her (obviously misplaced) optimism and bluster, the 66 year-old Mary was arrested and charged with murder. Mary Elizabeth Wilson always seemed far too cheerful to be a genuine grieving widow and that obviously led to her capture. As far as serial killers go, she was a terrible actor.

The prosecution at the trial found it rather difficult to prove a financial motive for the murders because Mary's husbands were not rich men in the least. In a way that made her crimes worse. She simply seemed to have developed an addiction to killing husbands - despite the somewhat paltry financial benefits these murders netted. Maybe she was simply another one of those serial poisoners who just liked going to funerals. Mary was initially sentenced to death at the trial but this sentence was then downsized to life in prison after an intervention by the Home Secretary. Mary Elizabeth Wilson died in prison in 1963. She was in her early seventies when she passed away.

RHONDA BELL MARTIN was born in 1907. Martin was an Alabama waitress who confessed to poisoning to death several members of her family in 1956. She killed three daughters, her mother and two husbands, mostly with rat poison. Martin also attempted to kill her fifth husband (and former step-son) but he survived and was left a paraplegic. The authorities were rather befuddled as to why she became a serial poisoner of relatives because the life insurance money and inheritances she accrued from these deaths was modest and barely covered all the funeral expenses.

Rhonda Belle Martin never really offered an explanation as to why she had killed most of her family. It has been suggested that she became addicted to the attention and sympathy she received whenever a relative died. Rhonda Belle Martin was rumbled when her latest husband survived his poisoning. An investigation soon deduced that many relatives of Martin had been poisoned. She also used ant poison and arsenic to kill her relatives. The poison was often put in coffee and then served up to the victim.

Rhonda Belle Martin was a rather unlikely serial killer as she was a plump and conservative looking bespectacled middle-aged housewife. Although she confessed to the murders her inability to explain why she had done them simply made her all the more baffling. Martin's lawyer tried to go for a plea of insanity in court and suggest that Rhonda had (as you do!) bumped off her husband so she could marry her step-son. In the end she was only tried for the death of her fourth husband. That was more than sufficient to give her the harshest of sentences.

It took a jury just over three hours to find her guilty. The sentence was death. Rhonda Belle Martin burst into tears at the verdict but was later quite stoic as her execution loomed. "Well, you've never seen anybody who was ready to sit down in the electric chair,' she said. 'But if that's what it's got to be, that's what it will be." She was executed in Alabama's electric chair on October 11, 1957. For her last meal she had a hamburger, mashed potatoes, cinnamon rolls and coffee.

Rhonda Belle Martin asked for her body to be donated to medical science in the hope that it might be of use in understanding future killers. 'At my death,' she wrote, 'whether it be a natural death of otherwise, I want my body to be given to some scientific institution to be used as they see fit, but especially to see if someone can find out why I committed the crimes I have committed. I can't understand it, for I had no reason whatsoever. There is definitely something wrong. Can't someone find it and save someone else the agony I have been through.'

DOROTHEA PUENTE was born Dorothea Helen Gray in 1929 in Redlands, California. She tends to be known as The Death House Landlady in true crime lore. Her childhood was absolutely awful. Her parents were alcoholics and she ended up in an orphanage where she suffered from sexual abuse. She was married in 1945 and had two children but the marriage didn't last for long and she sent the children away to live with relatives or be adopted. She also suffered a miscarriage.

In 1948, Dorothea Puente served a few months in jail for using bogus cheques. She got married again in 1952 but this was an obstreperous affair by all accounts. Puente was never faithful to her husband and alleged to fritter money away gambling. Puente went from fraud to prostitution in the years that followed and ended up running a brothel. In 1960 she was arrested for this and served another short prison sentence. In 1968, she married Roberto Jose Puente - from whom she got her infamous surname. Puente was much younger than his wife and the marriage only lasted sixteen months. He fled back to Mexico in the end.

Dorothea Puente switched careers again at this point and became a nurse's assistant. She eventually began managing boarding houses. Dorothea Puente ran a boarding house in Sacramento that housed elderly and mentally handicapped boarders. Puente was considered to be a pillar of the community and greatly respected. She looked like Grandma Walton and seemed to be the least threatening and most caring person imaginable. Nothing could be further from the actual truth though. Puente was responsible for cashing the social security cheques of her vulnerable tenants. Given her history of fraud this was a classic case of letting the fox run free in the hen house.

In 1978, Dorothea Puente was found guilty of cashing dozens of federal cheques that belonged to her tenants. However, she simply had to pay costs and go on probation. She was soon back to her old ways - only this time in more deadly fashion. Puente began to kill her boarders with drugs and then continue to cash their cheques after they had died. Because many of the boarders had no family she was able to get away with this for a time. She is believed to have made around $5000 a month from this scheme.

Ruth Monroe was Puente's first known murder victim. Monroe and Puente were actually business partners. Puente killed her with an overdose of codeine and Tyleno and then inherited a large sum of money from the estate of the victim. Some of Puente's victims were suffocated with a pillow. She put the body of one victim in a coffin and left it on a riverbank. Some of the victims were buried in Puente's basement. Neighbours sometimes detected a strange and pungent smell - which they complained about but obviously did not deduce was the result of dead bodies. You can hardly blame them. Who could have guessed that this seemingly sweet old lady was bumping off her boarders?

One victim even had the head and hands removed to lessen the chances of identification. The head and hands of this victim were never found. On investigating the disappearance of a man named Alberto Montoya, the police went to speak to Puente and noticed some loose soil on her property. No prizes for guessing why this soil was loose. Bodies were soon discovered. Amazingly, Puente wasn't a suspect at first and had been given permission by the police to go and get some coffee. She fled and booked into a hotel in Los Angeles under an assumed name. Puente was thankfully captured though and brought back to Sacramento to stand trial.

It took five years for the trial to take place - by which time Puente was 64 years-old. Puente's defence team tried to argue that she was simply a thief and fraudster who had never killed anyone. The prosecution and - crucially - the evidence said otherwise. They proved that a sedative named Dalmane had been found in several of the victims. It was even argued at the trial that Puente had paid former convicts to help her dispose of the bodies. Puente was charged with three counts of murder and sentenced to life in prison. She died in 2011 at the age of 82 and never confessed to her crimes.

TAMARA SAMSONOVA was born in 1947 in the city of Uzhur.

Samsonova tends to be known as The Granny Ripper in true crime circles for reasons that will soon become clear. As a young woman she got married and worked for a travel agency. However her husband mysteriously vanished in 2000. Given what we now know about Tamara Samsonova it doesn't seem like a tremendously outrageous notion to suggest that she might have killed him. Tamara Samsonova was arrested in 2015 after CCTV captured her struggling with various bags which were then found to contain human body parts. The body parts belonged to 79-year-old Valentina Ulanova - who Samsonova was supposed to be caring for.

Samsonova had poisoned the woman and then dismembered her body with a hacksaw. "I came home and put the whole pack of Phenazepamum - 50 pills - into her Olivier salad,' she told the police. 'She liked it very much. I woke up after 2am and she was lying on the floor. So I started cutting her to pieces. It was hard for me to carry her to the bathroom, she was fat and heavy. I did everything at the kitchen where she was lying." Samsonova was also captured in the footage with a saucepan which contained the head of her victim.

The motivation for the murder? Samsonova said she had got fed up with Valentina Ulanova because Valentina had a habit of not washing out the tea cups properly after she'd used them! Let that be a lesson to everyone. Wash out your mug after you've had a cup of tea! When the police arrested the 66 year-old Tamara Samsonova they found she had written diaries which featured extensive details on eleven murders she had carried out over the years. It was true too that the local area had had incidences of finding bags of human remains. Samsonova had dumped the headless body of Valentina Ulanova in a street before her arrest.

It was then established that in 2003, Tamara Samsonova had murdered a 44 year-old tenant who was staying with her. His headless and limb free body was also dumped in a street. "I killed my tenant Volodya," she told the police, "cut him to pieces in the bathroom with a knife and put the pieces of his body in plastic bags and threw them away in the different parts of Frunzensky District."

The police, on searching the home of Tamara Samsonova, found that she seemed to be obsessed with black magic. This was clearly a nutty and disturbed woman. The Russian media reported that Tamara Samsonova was also a cannibal who claimed to have removed and eaten the lungs of one of her victims.

Tamara Samsonova was sent to a psychiatric treatment hospital while the police began the complicated and difficult task of trying to establish just how many people she did or didn't kill. The answer to that question at this time is anyone's guess. We know that Tamara Samsonova killed at least three people but the true figure could be four times that if her diaries are to be believed.

CHAPTER THREE - POISONING GANGS

There have been numerous cases where poisoning collectives or gangs were formed. There have also been true crime cases where a family or relatives have got together to put a poisoning scheme into action. The motivation for most (but not all) of these cases, as we shall see, was money. AMELIA WINTERS was a woman at the heart of what became known as The Deptford Poisoning Cases. Winters, along with her daughter Elizabeth Frost, had insured the lives of 22 people for a total of £240 with the Liverpool Victoria Friendly Society. Five of these insured people then subsequently died in very suspicious circumstances.

The bizarre thing about the insurance law at the time was that one could insure a relative or tenant without them even being aware of this! If they then kicked the bucket you could simply go and collect the money. It is probably little wonder that so many murderers took advantage of the grisly possibilities offered up by the insurance laws of the day. Talk about a loophole. It was like an open invitation for the murderous minded who needed some money. The victims of Deptford Poisoning Cases included 11-year old Sydney Bolton - who was the son of a niece living with Winters, Elizabeth Frost's mother in law, and William Sutton, an old man who was distantly related to Winters.

The cause of death was put down severe stomach complaints by the doctor in all cases. Anyone who has read a lot of true crime history will know exactly what that means. It means they were poisoned. The other victims were a five year-old child and 63 year-old man. Amazingly, when Winters took out the policies she wasn't even asked what her relationship was to those she was seeking to insure. These deaths eventually attracted much suspicion and three exhumations took place. The medical examinations of the bodies found that the deceased had all ingested arsenic and that this was the probable cause of death. Amelia Winters was arrested in a case that attracted many headlines at the time. Her daughter Elizabeth was also arrested on suspicion of being an accomplice.

Amelia Winters passed away before the trial took place. She made a confession to her son before she died and admitted she had poisoned all those people. Winters said she regretted her actions and had no idea why she had done these crimes because she was financially comfortable anyway and hadn't even made that much money from the insurance collected for the deaths. Amelia also absolved her daughter of any blame.

Her daughter Elizabeth was cleared of murder charges but received a seven year prison sentence for forgery. Amelia Winters is suspected of several other murders which did not come up in the investigation. She clearly poisoned an awful lot of people. The case of Amelia Winters led to a revision in the laws regarding life insurance. The authorities had obviously noticed that the laws as they were were almost like an open invitation for murderers and poisoners to exploit them for their own ends. Amelia Winters was buried in Brockley cemetery in Lewisham. An angry mob had threatened to disrupt her funeral and dig her up so the burial had to take place in private and be kept secret.

THE BLACK WIDOWS OF LIVERPOOL were sisters Catherine Flannagan and Margaret Higgins. Catherine was the elder sister by about fourteen years. The two women are thought to have come from Ireland although true crime scholars don't believe this was ever completely verified. Some have even suggested they came from Scotland. They originally ran an ale house when they came to Liverpool but ran foul of the law and the place was closed down. One of the misdeeds was to open on Sunday - something that was definitely not allowed in those days. They needed to find a new way to make a living after this so became money lenders and got involved in burial societies.

Burial societies historically existed in England and elsewhere and were for the purpose of providing, by voluntary subscriptions, for the funeral expenses of the husband, wife or child of a member, or of the widow of a deceased member. The sisters eventually ran a rooming house. Living in the house were Catherine's son John and a lodger named Thomas Higgins and his daughter Mary. Another lodger was Patrick Jennings and his daughter Margaret. It didn't take long for some strange things to begin to happen in this house.

Catherine's son John died quite suddenly at the age of 22 in 1880. As a result of his death, Catherine was given £70 by the burial society. This was a more than decent sum of money for the time. A few years later Margaret Flannagan and Thomas Higgins got married and she became Margaret Higgins. Tragedy struck though when his eight year-old daughter Mary died only weeks after the wedding. Margaret naturally collected some money from the burial society after Mary passed away. You could say that these two sisters were beginning to become a trifle suspicious. This was only heightened by the next death to strike the house.

In 1883, nineteen year-old Margaret Jennings, the daughter of the other lodger, also died suddenly. By now there was a lot of local gossip about all these apparently healthy youngsters suddenly dropping dead at this cursed rooming house. The sisters decided to move to a new house in an attempt to escape from the gossip and, in September 1883, Thomas Higgins fell ill and died two days later. He was 45. His death was put down to dysentery but that was obviously not the case at all. It transpired that insurance policies had been taken out on Thomas and his death was simply too suspicious to ignore - especially in light of the other deaths that had surrounded the sisters in recent years.

The funeral of Thomas Higgins was actually halted by the police so they could examine the body. It was found to contain arsenic. It was the brother of Thomas Higgins who kicked up the biggest fuss and prodded the authorities to investigate. He was highly suspicious because his brother had been in very good health. He was also highly suspicious when he learned that the two sisters had collected £100 from various policies when Thomas died. Margaret was arrested immediately but Catherine tried to flee. She was eventually arrested a week later. All of the victims were exhumed in the end and found to have been poisoned.

The sisters are believed to have concocted their poison by soaking flypaper (which contained arsenic) in water. The two sisters went on trial at the Liverpool Assizes in February 1884. Though they confessed to the murders, Catherine claimed that the poisonings were part a wider conspiracy involving the local burial society and they were operating with others. Catherine claimed the real ringleaders were others and not them. Given how many crazy female poisoners there were in this era, that doesn't sound like an implausible theory at all. Despite some circumstantial evidence though this was never proven. On the 3rd of March 1884, the two sisters were hung at Kirkdale Prison. A crowd of around 1,000 turned up to watch. As far as public executions from this era go, it was a rather disappointing turn out.

Amelia Sach (born 1873) and Annie Walters (born 1869) were two women who became known as THE FINCHLEY BABY FARMERS. These two women conspired to murder babies in order to make money from the Victorian practice of baby farming. Amelia Sach started a business where babies who needed adoption could be left with her for a fee. Annie Walters would then poison the babies and dispose of them. Sach was married and a fairly respected woman (at least to the unsuspecting world at large) while much less is known about the background of Walters. Walters was deemed to be of very low intelligence and was the one who did the 'dirty work' in this evil scheme.

Many of the babies that these two women dealt with were said to be the illegitimate children of servant girls and maids. There was a great stigma to having a child out of wedlock in the Victorian era and this created a need for women to look after unwanted infants until a home could be found for them. This allowed evil women like Amelia Dyer and the Finchley Baby Farmers to take advantage. They would collect the fee for taking in a baby and then kill the baby so that they didn't incur any further expense looking after them.

Chlorodyne was used to poison the babies. Chlorodyne contains a combination of active ingredients, including laudanum (a preparation of opium), chloroform, and cannabis indica resin. Chlorodyne was originally developed in the 19th century by English physician John Collis Browne.

It should be noted though that the vast majority of baby farmers were kind and decent women who looked after the babies as if they were their own children. The likes of Sach and Walters were tragic aberrations. What made it quite difficult to weed out murderous baby farmers was the fact that in this era a lot of infants and children died of disease or illness anyway. If an infant died, although tragic, it wasn't something that was especially uncommon.

It was the stupidity of Annie Walters that brought this evil duo to the attention of the authorities. Walters took a baby girl (which was actually a boy but Walters didn't seem to have noticed) home with her and showed the child off to the neighbours. However, the neighbours couldn't fail to notice that the infant disappeared soon after. Walters did the same thing again with a little girl and the authorities decided to investigate. It was rather odd and chilling that Walters seemed to be affectionate towards these infants in the company of her neighbours but then killed them as part of the baby farming scheme. Talk about Jekyll & Hyde.

The two women were (despite their predictable claims of innocence) sentenced to death for murdering the babies in their charge. The hangman who executed the two women later wrote -

'These two women were baby farmers of the worst kind and were both repulsive in type. They had literally to be carried to the scaffold and protested to the end against their sentences.' The bodies of Amelia Sach and Annie Walters were buried in Holloway Prison after their execution. When the prison was rebuilt in 1971, the bodies had to be exhumed and moved elsewhere.

THE ANGEL MAKERS OF NAGYREV were a group of woman in Hungry who poisoned to death a large collection of husbands in the village of Nagyrév. How many they killed is not known for sure. Some estimates claim they poisoned 300 men. Even the most conservative estimates though would put the number of victims at around forty or fifty. The ringleader of this group was a midwife named Júlia Fazekas. At the time, the tradition in this village was that the parents of women chose the husband for their daughter. This meant that teenage brides were married off to men that they hadn't chosen themselves and in many cases didn't like very much.

This custom obviously entrapped a lot of women in unhappy marriages. Sometimes they were married off to men who turned out to be abusive or drunks. This was mitigated somewhat by the First World War. Women in unhappy marriages quite enjoyed the fact that their husbands were away fighting and in many cases enjoyed affairs. These affairs were much more to their liking because, unlike their marriages, they had actually been allowed to choose their lovers themselves. However, after the war the husbands all came home and a number of women found themselves back in the unhappy marriage they hadn't even wanted in the first place.

It was Júlia Fazekas who came up with a solution to the problem of unhappy wives in arranged marriages. She suggested they simply murder their husbands by boiling flypaper and skimming off the arsenic residue. The women in the village soon got the hang of the poisoning lark the persuasive Fazekas had proposed and local husbands began dropping like (ahem) flies. There was only one problem though. They didn't stop at husbands. Soon they were poisoning parents, lovers, and even sons. Generally anyone that annoyed them got a dose of arsenic.

Nagyrév became known as 'murder district' because there were so many sudden deaths in the area. Now, you might wonder why none of this was raised any suspicion and why no action was taken by the authorities for so many years. There were a number of reasons for this. The first is that the village didn't actually have a doctor. Júlia Fazekas, as a midwife, was actually considered to be the main medical expert in the village and she obviously wasn't going to say or do anything that would threaten the dark secret of this town as she was the mastermind behind it.

The second reason is that the cousin of Júlia Fazekas was the village clerk in charge of handling the death certificates. Fazekas obviously, with her influence over the clerk, made sure that these deaths were put down to natural causes. The poisonings went on for over a decade until they were put to a stop. There are a number of conflicting explanations for why the women of Nagyrév were finally rumbled. Some say that a doctor visited the village and found arsenic in the body of a dead man. Other reports say that some of the wives in the village were caught in the act of poisoning husbands.

Another claim is that one of the villagers exposed the dark secret of the village by writing an anonymous letter to a newspaper. However it happened though, the murders in the village were eventually uncovered and a number of exhumations took place. Twelve women in the village received prison sentences and two were executed. Thirty eight women in all were arrested. As for Júlia Fazekas, she didn't stick around to explain herself or take the blame. She hung herself in 1929.

THE PHILADELPHIA POISON RING ring refers to a criminal organisation that operated in Philadelphia during the late 19th and early 20th centuries. The ring was involved in various illegal activities, including the production and distribution of poisonous substances, which were often used for nefarious purposes. The ring consisted of a network of individuals who manufactured and sold toxic substances, such as arsenic and cyanide, to be used for murder or sabotage. They supplied these poisons to anyone willing to pay, including criminals who wanted to eliminate rivals, spouses seeking to poison their partners, or people looking to commit insurance fraud.

One of the most notorious figures associated with the Philadelphia poison ring was Louisa Cody, a German immigrant who was known as the "Poison Queen." Cody was a central figure in the organisation and became notorious for her role in various poisoning cases. She would often provide lethal substances to clients, disguised as medicine or other harmless substances. The activities of the Philadelphia poison ring came to light when a series of suspicious deaths and illnesses occurred in the city.

The police launched an investigation, which eventually led them to the ring's operations. In 1909, a trial was held, and several members of the organisation, including Louisa Cody, were convicted for their involvement in the illegal activities. The Philadelphia poison ring case exposed the dangers of unregulated substances and led to stricter regulations on the sale of toxic materials. It also highlighted the need for better forensic methods to detect poisoning cases and brought attention to the rising issue of poison-related crimes during that time.

THE LAINZ ANGELS OF DEATH were Maria Gruber, Irene Leidolf, Stephanija Meyer, and Waltraud Wagner. This quartet were Austrian nurses who murdered dozens of patients at a Vienna hospital by giving them overdoses of morphine or putting water into their lungs. Waltraud Wagner was the first of the women to kill but they all conspired and worked together in the end when it came to killing patients.

Three of the women were very young (Maria Gruber in particular was only a teenager) but Stephanija Meyer was in her forties and her age made her the most charismatic of the group. She arguably wielded the most influence. The nurses would pinch the nose of victims and pour water in them. Many of these patients were very feeble and unable to struggle. Few of these patients were terminally ill and they would have lived to leave hospital were it not for these evil women.

Waltraud Wagner, who recruited the other nurses into this heartless activity, had classic symptoms of God complex - a familiar trait of serial killers who work in the medical profession. Wagner loved the sense of power she had over these patients and clearly enjoyed taking lives. The Lainz Angels of Death were captured when they were overheard bragging about their murders in a pub. They were thankfully taken into custody very quickly.

It later transpired that investigators had raised alarm bells about a suspicious death at the hospital in 1988 but couldn't go very far in their investigation because of the lack of cooperation from the hospital (who clearly wanted to brush the suspicious death under the carpet lest there be any legal complications). The women confessed to over forty murders but the true figure is impossible to say. Some accounts of this case they might have potentially killed over a hundred people.

Wagner was convicted of 15 murders, 17 attempts, and two counts of assault. She was sentenced to life in prison. Irene Leidolf also received a life sentence for five murders. Wagner and Leidolf tried to claim the murders had been mercy killings of terminally ill patients but this simply didn't wash when subjected to sustained scrutiny in court. Meyer and Gruber received twenty years in prison for manslaughter and attempted murder. Meyer and Gruber were released fairly soon and given new identities. That was surprising but even more controversial was the release of Wagner and Leidolf in 2008 for 'good behaviour' in prison.

The preposterously early release of these women caused outrage in Austria and made both the media and public alike wonder if the country's justice system was too soft and forgiving. It hardly must have seemed fair to the relatives of the victims that these four awful women had barely spent any time in prison at all for their dreadful and chilling crimes. It is amazing really to think that they were all released from prison so soon - as if their crimes had been petty or not that serious. Off the top of my head I can't think of many more serious crimes than murdering helpless patients in a hospital.

GWENDOLYN GRAHAM & CATHY WOOD became known as The Lethal Lovers after killing five patients in Michigan's Alpine Manor. This diabolical duo were nursing aides and lovers. The victims were - Mae Mason, 79, Edith Cole, 89, Marguerite Chambers, 60, Myrtle Luce, 95, and Belle Burkhard, 74. Graham and Wood first met in 1986 and moved in together. They killed their first victim at the start of 1987 and got away with it because the death was deemed to have been as a result of natural causes.

Graham and Wood wanted to choose victims whose names spelled out 'murder' as part of a sick private game but they abandoned this plan in the end because it proved too difficult. The patients were suffocated by the duo. They believed that by killing together they would cement an unbreakable bond. The murderous duo eventually went their separate ways though and this split led to their downfall. That unbreakable bond obviously wasn't as unbreakable as they thought. Gwendolyn Graham began a relationship with another nurse and then moved to Texas.

The crimes of Wood and Graham came to light because of Wood's ex-husband. Cathy Wood had confessed the murders to him and he went to the police. When the police interviewed Wood she confessed to the murders and said they suffocated the patients with washcloths. Wood testified against Graham at the trial and as a consequence Graham was convicted of first-degree murder of all five victims and handed five life sentences. Wood received a sentence based on her guilty plea of one charge of conspiracy to commit murder and one charge of second-degree murder.

Cathy Wood was granted parole by the Michigan Department of Corrections in 2018 and in 2020 she was released. The relatives of the victims were very upset by this and believe that Wood downplayed her own role in the murders to get a lesser charge than Gwendolyn Graham. Some retrospectives of this case have argued that Wood was the most dangerous of the duo and the brains and driving force behind the whole murderous operation. Gwendolyn Graham, in a prison interview, said that Cathy wood was 'evil' and expressed astonishment that her partner in crime was now a free woman.

Retired police officer Roger Kaliniak, who was involved in the case when the two women were investigated and arrested, said he was rather surprised to learn that Cathy Wood had been released. "She's a serial killer and she could do it again, and most of them do," he said. "I believe that Cathy Wood was the mastermind, she was the one that was pulling strings on Gwendolyn Graham. Gwendolyn Graham handled the dirty work and Cathy Wood was the brains behind it. "

Court documents from the trial suggested that the two women tried to kill at least ten patients in all. The only crumb of comfort from this awful case is that the two women went their separate ways fairly quickly. The body count would have been considerably higher if they hadn't. Graham and Woods were later the inspiration for a 2016 episode of American Horror Story where two nurses named Miranda and Bridget decide to kill their patients.

THE CHICAGO TYLENOL MURDERS refers to a series of poisonings that took place in the Chicago area in 1982. Seven people died after consuming Tylenol capsules that had been laced with cyanide. The incident began on September 29, 1982, when three people died shortly after taking Extra-Strength Tylenol capsules purchased from different stores in the Chicago suburbs. This was followed by four more deaths in the following days. Authorities discovered that the capsules had been tampered with, and cyanide was found in the products.

The investigation led by the Federal Bureau of Investigation (FBI) and the Illinois State Police resulted in a massive recall of Tylenol capsules that affected millions of bottles, costing Johnson & Johnson, the manufacturer, over $100 million. The company took immediate steps to ensure customer safety, including introducing tamper-evident packaging. Despite an extensive investigation, the person responsible for the murders was never identified or apprehended. The case remains unsolved to this day. However, the incident had a significant impact on public safety measures, leading to stricter regulations and tamper-proof packaging for over-the-counter medications.

TAMARA IVANYUTINA was born in the Ukrainian SSR in 1841. Ivanyutina has a small if rather unwelcome place in history as she was the last woman to be executed in the Soviet Union. The pretty odd thing about Tamara Ivanyutina is that most of her family seemed to be serial killers. If you got on the wrong side of them they would simply slip some thallium into your food and drink. Tamara's parents are said to have once poisoned a cousin for the high crime of spreading some idle gossip about them!

The family as a collective are said to have poisoned over forty people and around thirteen of these incidents turned out to be fatal. As for Tamara alone, she is generally credited with nine solo murders. She killed her first husband so she could have his apartment and when she got married again she killed her father-in-law because she wanted his house. Poisoning was considered to be something of a must have skill in the Ivanyutina family. Tamara even tutored her sister Nina in the art of poisoning because her sister had an annoying husband she wanted to bump off.

In the mid 1980s, Tamara got a job as a dishwasher in a school in the Podolsk district of Kiev. As you might fear and expect, a prolific and compulsive poisoner like Tamara Ivanyutina working in a school was never going to have much of a happy ending. In 1987, staff and pupils at the school where Tamara worked began to mysteriously fall ill. Two children and two adults died very quickly. The dietitian at the school had been poisoned a few weeks before. It came as no surprise to later learn that Tamara Ivanyutina was said to loathe this dietician because she was snooty and rude to humble school dishwashers.

An investigation into the deaths and illnesses at the school looked into the food because the survivors were now in hospital with severe stomach problems. The police also exhumed the body of the dietitian who had died and found traces of thallium. The investigation now drew up a list of all staff at the school who had access to the kitchen. Tamara Ivanyutina was on that list and had her house searched where - sure enough - investigators found a bottle of poison that matched the poison found in the victim. She was arrested and found to have got the job in the school with fake ID (that hid her past criminal convictions).

The investigation further revealed that the Ivanyutina family procured poison from the Geological Institute and that most of the family had killed people. Tamara's sister got fifteen years, her father and mother – respectively ten and thirteen years. Tamara was sentenced to death and executed in 1987. The family tried to bribe the authorities into letting them off but that obviously didn't work. Tamara was very reluctant to offer any confessions but she did seem to imply that she poisoned the children because they always irritated her by not stacking the chairs correctly in the canteen after lunch. Let that be a lesson to all schoolchildren. Stack those chairs tidily because you never know who might be working in the kitchen!

THE TOKYO SUBWAY SARIN ATTACK, also known as the Tokyo sarin gas attack, occurred on March 20, 1995. It was a domestic terrorist attack carried out by the religious cult called Aum Shinrikyo. The cult's nutty leader, Shoko Asahara, aimed to overthrow the Japanese government and spark an apocalypse. During the morning rush hour, members of Aum Shinrikyo dispersed the deadly nerve gas sarin in the Tokyo subway system. Sarin is a highly toxic nerve agent developed for military use. It is classified as a chemical weapon and is considered a weapon of mass destruction. Sarin gas is a clear, colorless liquid that evaporates quickly into a vapor and can be inhaled or absorbed through the skin. It affects the nervous system by inhibiting an enzyme called acetylcholinesterase, which is responsible for breaking down the neurotransmitter acetylcholine. This leads to an excessive build-up of acetylcholine in the body, causing overstimulation of the nervous system.

Exposure to sarin gas can result in a wide range of symptoms, including respiratory distress, blurred vision, drooling, excessive sweating, muscle twitching, seizures, paralysis, and ultimately, death due to respiratory failure. Even at low levels of exposure, sarin can cause long-term health effects and neurological damage. Sarin gas has been used in several instances of chemical warfare and terrorist attacks. The Tokyo gang targeted five trains, all converging at the busy subway station of Kasumigaseki, near the Japanese government's administrative offices. The attackers punctured plastic bags filled with liquid sarin with umbrella tips, then left the bags placed on the trains' floors. The sarin quickly evaporated, filling the subway cars with the odorless and colorless gas.

The attack resulted in the death of 13 people and caused thousands of injuries, ranging from mild to severe. Panic and chaos spread throughout the subway system as passengers experienced symptoms such as difficulty breathing, blurred vision, dizziness, and nausea. Emergency services were overwhelmed, and some victims had to be treated on the streets. It took several days to fully decontaminate the affected subway stations and trains. The Tokyo Subway sarin attack led to a significant crackdown on Aum Shinrikyo. The cult's leader, Shoko Asahara, and several other members, were apprehended and later sentenced to death. The incident prompted greater scrutiny of religious and doomsday cults in Japan, as well as improvements in security and counter-terrorism measures.

THE ANTIFREEZE MURDERS refers to a case in Springfield, Missouri, in 2012. A woman named Diane Staudte, who was a trained nurse, murdered her 61 year-old husband Mark and 26 year-old son Shaun by putting antifreeze in soft drinks. She also tried to murder her 24 year-old daughter Sarah in the same fashion but Sarah survived - though she was left seriously ill and now requires care. Diane Staudte also planned to murder her 9 year-old daughter Briana but - mercifully - she was rumbled before she got around to that. Here's the kicker in this grim tale. Diana had an accomplice - her 22 year-old daughter Rachel.

Rachel was Diane's favourite child and mother and daughter basically conspired to bump off the entire family. The motive for the murders was that Diane Staudte had grown to loathe her husband. Mr Staudte was in a local music band and wasn't bringing much money into the house. Diane Staudte also considered her children (aside from Rachel) to be a burden she could happily do without. Shaun had autism and still lived at home. Sarah had student debts and had moved back home too. Diane was fed up with these grown children still living at home and not contributing any money. Rachel was more than happy to go along with these plans to poison the family.

Oddly, the duo didn't attract much suspicion at first despite these sudden deaths but it didn't take too long for them to attract attention. Friends of Mr Staudte noticed that Diane didn't seem to be upset at all by his death. At the funeral she acted as if it was a party rather than a sad event. Friends and relatives of the family also found it strange that there was no memorial or any sort of service at all for Shaun. Diane seemed very happy to everyone - which was bizarre behaviour for a woman who had just lost her husband and son. Rachel was behaving oddly too. She posted a picture of her mother on Facebook and talked about how 'chilled' her mother was.

Diane collected an insurance payout from the murders and made plans to move house and go on holiday. However, a pastor at the local church contacted the police to raise his concerns about Diane's behaviour. The pastor was suspicious because he had known Mark and Shaun. They'd both seemed perfectly healthy to him before they suddenly died. The pastor had also noted that Diane had showed no sign of being saddened by the deaths. Quite the contrary. She seemed happy.

Not long after the attempted murder of Sarah, Diane was arrested.

Rachel was arrested the nest day. This evil duo had no option but to confess. Diane got life without parole. In return for testifying against her mother, Rachel was given life but with the possibility of parole after 42 years. The youngest daughter Briana was taken into foster care. Sarah was left damaged by the attempted poisoning but did survive. She has talked about the case on her Facebook page.

Diane Staudte recently did a television interview in which she said she was innocent and may have been poisoned too. This was of course hogwash. There is no evidence she was poisoned and plenty of evidence that she was the poisoner. Rachel, who pled guilty to two charges of second degree murder, has recently attempted to overturn this plea deal by saying she wasn't made aware of her rights at the time and had a 'fear' of men which meant she was terrified of the police detectives and just agreed to anything they said. Rachel's appeals would appear to be fairly pointless one would imagine. Even if her claims are true they are not going to turn her loose are they? Diane and Rachel are now paying the price for the evil things they did. It's fair to say that no one has much sympathy for them.

CHAPTER FOUR - BLACK WIDOWS

One of the salient differences between male and female serial killers is that a lot of male serial killers are motivated by a desire to satiate sick sexual fantasies and desires. This doesn't happen so much with female killers (though there are a few exceptions). Female serial killers, or poisoners as the case is in this book, tend to be motivated by money or love - in that they want to bump off someone for money or to make room for a new lover. ELIZABETH RIDGEWAY was born in the late 17th century on a farm outside Ibstock, Leicestershire. Elizabeth lived with her mother for most of her young life. In fact she was nearly thirty when this relationship came to an end. The cause of the split? Well, Elizabeth murdered her mother by means of poison after they had a falling out. She used white mercury or arsenic to poison her victims. You've probably heard of the term mercury poisoning. Elizabeth took mercury poisoning to the next level.

After the death of her mother, Elizabeth had to get a job and ended up becoming a maid in a house not too far way. It is said that she fell out with a fellow servant there and so poisoned him with arsenic. Elizabeth Ridgeway was definitely the last person you'd want to get into an argument with. You could say that she was someone who knew how to hold a grudge! Her method for poisoning someone was the usual one practiced by numerous poisoners through the decades (and indeed centuries) - food and drink. She would slip poison into porridge that someone would eat or simply put some in a cup of tea and give it to the victim.

Elizabeth Ridgeway was said to be an attractive woman and she soon had a number of men vying for her attention. One such man was John King. Elizabeth gave King the impression that she was willing to become his wife but when she decided she didn't want to go through with this she simply poisoned him to rid herself of this problem. In 1683 she married Thomas Ridgeway. Elizabeth had chosen Thomas Ridgeway because he was wealthy. Guess what happened to Thomas Ridgeway? That's right. Death by poisoned broth. He was killed three weeks into the marriage.

It was at this stage though that the activities of Elizabeth Ridgeway attracted suspicion. Apprentices of Thomas Ridgeway recalled that he had complained of his broth being gritty and strange when he ate his fateful doom laden meal (which had occurred in a church of all places). The apprentices noticed that when Elizabeth served them some porridge soon after it also had a gritty texture. They were too suspicious to eat any of it and deduced what was happening. Elizabeth was trying to kill them to secure their silence. Once Elizabeth realised they were onto her she tried to bribe them in return for silence but they reported her to Thomas Ridgeway's relatives.

A medical examination of the body of Thomas Ridgeway confirmed that he had been poisoned. Cruentation was used to test Elizabeth's guilt. What is cruentention? According to definitions.net -

'Cruentation (Latin: "ius cruentationis" or "Ius feretri sine sandapilae") was one of the medieval methods of finding proof against a suspected murderer. The common belief was that the body of the victim would spontaneously bleed in the presence of the murderer.'

Elizabeth Ridgeway was found guilty and sentenced to death. As this was 1684, the method was execution was death by burning at the stake! There were some attempts to reduce her sentence and show a little more mercy (burning at the stake is, to say the least, pretty extreme) but it was the refusal of Elizabeth to offer confessions to a local clergyman that sealed her fate. She had no interest in begging God for forgiveness.

MARY ANN COTTON was born in Sunderland in 1832. She tends to be known as The Black Widow in true crime lore. Cotton has sometimes been called Britain's first serial killer. It's safe to say that if you were ever offered a cup of tea by Mary Ann Cotton you'd be advised to decline unless you enjoy a large dose of arsenic in your PG Tips. Her childhood was fairly uneventful save for her father dying in a mining accident. She spent some time in a boarding school and was said to be a sensible girl who always took a great pride in her appearance. This last quality was evident in her choice of profession. Mary trained to become a dressmaker.

In 1852, Mary married a man named William Mowbray. They had several children but few of them survived. Not all of these births were registered so it was difficult to keep track of exactly how many children they had and how many died. In those days the sad premature death of babies and infants was not uncommon so these deaths were not considered suspicious. Mary's husband William died in 1865 because of a stomach ailment. William was insured and Mary received a nice little payment upon his death as a result. Mary's second husband was George Ward. He also died though - once again allowing Mary to collect an insurance payment. The cause of death was cited as cholera but the suddenness of his departure from this vale of tears was rather surprising.

Husband number three for Mary was a widower named James Robinson. Meanwhile, Mary's mother died suddenly after complaining of stomach pains. Yes, you might say that all these sudden deaths in relation to Mary were becoming rather too suspicious. Mary's daughter and two of Robinson's children (from his previous marriage) then all suddenly died in quick succession. James Robinson had noticed at this juncture how Mary kept trying to persuade him to take out life insurance. He decided to boot her out of the house after discovering that she had been pawning his valuables and running up debts.

In 1870, Mary nabbed husband number four when she married Frederick Cotton (from whom she obviously got her last name). Mary was pretty destitute by this point after the collapse of her last marriage and so was desperate to find a new husband - preferably one who was minted. This new marriage was actually illegal because she wasn't even officially divorced from her last husband. Mary wasn't the greatest wife in the world it has to be said. She found out that an old flame named Joseph Nattrass lived nearby and so went off to woo him. As for Frederick Cotton, you can probably guess what happened to him. That's right. He died of a stomach complaint.

Frederick Jr, the child of her last husband, then suddenly died as did Joseph Nattrass - who was Mary's lodger at the time. In 1872, one of Mary Cotton's surviving stepchildren Charles Cotton died suddenly and mysteriously. Mary had told a parish official that Charles 'was in the way' of her future plans. When the apparently healthy Charles dropped dead, the local parish official became highly suspicious (not before time you might argue!) of Mary.

Mary tried to collect the life insurance on Charles but the authorities would not release the money until a medical investigation had taken place. When the body of Charles Cotton was exhumed, arsenic was found in his system. At the trial which followed, Mary was sentenced to death but insisted she was innocent. 'After conviction,' wrote The Times, 'the wretched woman exhibited strong emotion but this gave place in a few hours to her habitual cold, reserved demeanour and while she harbours a strong conviction that the royal clemency will be extended towards her, she staunchly asserts her innocence of the crime that she has been convicted of.' Mary Ann Cotton was hanged at Durham County Gaol in March 1873. The hanging was rather botched and she ended up slowly choking to death on the rope. Of Mary Ann Cotton's thirteen estimated children, only two survived her. She had killed the vast majority of her family.

GESCHE GOTTFRIED was born born Gesche Margarethe Timm in Germany. She was known as The Angel of Bremen and poisoned fifteen people to death. It made no difference to Gottfried who the person was. She happily poisoned friends and relatives. Gesche Gottfried grew up in a large and poor family and always felt rather unloved. It is speculated that she later developed Munchausen syndrome by proxy (MSP). In medical terms, this is defined as a disorder in which the caretaker of a person either makes up fake symptoms or causes real symptoms to make it appear as though the person is injured or ill. The term by proxy means through a substitute.

Though MSP is primarily a mental illness, it is also considered a form of abuse. Many people with MSP exaggerate or lie about a person's symptoms to get attention. They may also create symptoms by poisoning food, withholding food, or causing an infection. Some people may even have a person undergo painful or risky tests and procedures to try to gain sympathy from their family members or community.

Gesche Gottfried poisoned to death, amongst others, two husbands, her mother and father, two daughters and a son, her brother, a fiancé, and numerous friends. She enjoyed the sympathy that people gave her as a result of these deaths. They obviously had no idea that Gottfried was killing these people so showered her with sympathy and support each time she 'suffered' the loss of a loved one. She would mix rat poison in animal fat and then slip this into the food of her victims. She often killed people slowly by giving them small amounts of poison at a time. Once the victim started to become ill, Gottfriend would of course volunteer to care for them.

Part of the motivation for these murders was obviously money as Gesche collected a number of inheritances as a result of so many relatives dying. She was creative with her methods and once poisoned someone through a dish of shellfish. Her exploits came to an end when one would be victim noticed some white power on food that Gesche had given him. He consulted a local doctor about this and the substance was identified as arsenic. Gesche was arrested in 1828. She was 43 years-old at the time. Gesche Gottfried was sentenced to death by decapitation and beheaded on April the 21st 1831. This was the last public execution ever carried out in the city of Bremen.

CATHERINE WILSON was born in Boston in 1822. Many of her crimes took place in London though so she tends to be lumped in with British serial killers. You could probably call Catherine Wilson a transatlantic serial killer. Catherine was a housekeeper and nurse who would poison those she was caring for. Naturally, she would make sure they named her in the will before they kicked the bucket.

Her first victim is believed to have been Captain Peter Mawer in Boston. This old man died in 1854 in Catherine's care. Before he died he changed his will so she got the money. Catherine moved to London and became the mistress of a man named James Dixon. Dixon, though not old at all, died while Catherine was treating him for his alcohol dependence. Catherine was lodging in the home of Mrs Maria Soames at the time. Mrs Soames suddenly fell ill and died a few days later. Catherine told everyone it must have been a suicide.

In 1859, Catherine went back to Boston and killed a woman named Mrs Jackson. Jackson, rather suspiciously, died only days after a huge amount of money had been withdrawn from her bank account. Catherine's next victim was the aunt of the late James Dixon. Mrs Dixon suddenly fell ill and died while with Catherine. When Mrs Dixon's distraught husband turned up, Catherine even managed to get some money out of him by pretending that she'd lent the late Mrs Dixon a considerable sum of cash!

The career of Catherine Wilson as a serial killer came to an end in 1862 when she was in London looking after a woman named Sarah Carnell. Sarah was given a drink by Catherine but found it strangely bitter and so - on instinct - spat it out. The liquid seemed to have a corrosive effect on the carpet. Sarah's husband burst in to see what all the fuss was about and Catherine fled. She was eventually apprehended and tried to pretend that she had unwittingly been sold acid by the chemist and the order must have got mixed up. A likely story indeed.

This defence didn't stand up to much scrutiny because it transpired that Catherine had persuaded Sarah to rewrite her will before she gave her the acid. No prizes for guessing who the new beneficiary of the money was going to be should Sarah Carnell shuffle off this mortal coil. Once they had Catherine Wilson in custody, the police looked into her background and saw all manner of suspicious deaths linked to her. It is generally estimated that she might have killed around seven people. Colchicum and arsenic were her chemicals of choice when it came to murder.

In 1862, Catherine Wilson was put on trial for the murder of Maria Soames and found guilty. This one charge was enough to secure a death sentence. Catherine was hanged outside the Old Bailey that same day. The public in those days clearly loved nothing more than a good execution because 20,000 people turned up to watch. It was the last public execution involving a woman to take place in England.

BELLE GUNNESS (born 1859) was a Norwegian woman who moved to the United States in the late 19th century. She had a farm in Indiana but any men who went to this farm were seemingly never seen again. Belle Gunness put an ad in the paper looking for a husband but this was one ad you didn't want to respond to. Her life and death is still shrouded in some mystery but there is enough evidence to suggest that Belle Gunness was a very deadly woman and best avoided unless you wanted an early grave.

When she first moved to America she married a Norwegian man and they opened a store. There were four children too. The husband died in a store fire though - which was handy for Belle because she got an insurance payout. She used the money to buy a farm in Indiana and got married again. The new husband didn't last very long though. Mere months later he was dead in what Belle described (with some understatement) as an unfortunate meat grinder accident. Amazingly though, the authorities still didn't seem to suspect any foul play when it came to this mysterious woman.

Belle then placed an ad in the newspaper in an attempt to find another husband. Many men went to the farm after reading the ad but none of them were seen again. You probably had better odds of surviving a tour of duty in Afghanistan than you did of a trip to the farm of Belle Gunness. She is said to have used strychnine on some of her victims. In 1908 the farm burned down and the police found the remains of eleven victims - which included Belle's children and a woman's head. Did Belle die in the blaze or did she stage the whole thing to escape? The jury is still out. No one knows what happened. It is often reported that the head found on the farm belonged to Belle Gunness but this was never verified for sure.

Naturally there were unverified sightings of Belle Gunness in the years that followed but her true fate remains a mystery. Ray Lamphere, who worked on Belle's farm, was a suspect in the murders but he was never actually charged (except for arson). It seems plausible (given that many allege he was Belle's lover) that Lamphere might have been an accomplice. Perhaps he decided to kill Belle in the end. Locals who live near the old farm of Belle Gunness often report it to be haunted now. They say you can often hear screams coming the site from where the victims of Belle Gunness perished.

MARIA SWANENBURG was born in Gorinchem, Netherlands, 1839. Known as Goeie Mie (good morning), she is sometimes alleged to have poisoned over one hundred people. Those who have researched her story in Holland believe this figure is exaggerated but there's no doubt that - at the very least - she was a prolific poisoner with dozens of victims. Even a conservative victim estimate would put her near the top table of female serial killers. Swanenburg killed by slipping arsenic into food and drink. One of her favourite methods was to slip poison into a bowl of porridge. Yes, we can safely say that Maria Swanenburg was the last person in the world you'd want to have some breakfast with.

She poisoned both her mother and father and sixteen relatives in all. Swanenburg lived in a destitute sort of area and often worked as a babysitter. Because this area was very poor and people were dying of disease, poverty, and natural causes all the time, her activities didn't really provoke much suspicion for a while. Swanenburg was never suspected by anyone who knew her because she was considered by everyone to be a kind and generous person. She had a matronly sort of air and was like a beloved aunt in the community. Her motivation for the murders was, in some cases, money. She would poison relatives with life insurance policies and steal the money.

She also took the possessions and valuables of others she murdered. Here's the strange thing though. Maria Swanenburg also poisoned people with no life insurance and no money. It was established that even when she stood to make not a single penny from a victim she still poisoned them. She just seemed to be addicted to the act of poisoning someone to death. The poison was something she'd purchased easily and legally in a store as a way to remove bedbugs. Swanenburg's killing spree came to an end when three members of a family died in suspiciously similar circumstances and a doctor smelled a rat and decided to investigate. The bodies of the family victims were exhumed and examined - verifying that they had been poisoned. Swanenburg was linked to this family and swiftly arrested. Maria Swanenburg confessed to the murders and was taken into permanent custody.

The case received tremendous press coverage in the Netherlands.

There were lynch mobs out for Maria Swanenburg's blood when the trial began. Her only words during the trial were an appeal for mercy. Swanenburg was sentenced to life in prison and died behind bars in 1915 at the age of 75. It is impossible to tell how many people she tried to poison in her exploits as a serial killer. At least fifty people either became mysteriously ill or died in the area while she was active.

As a result of the Maria Swanenburg case, the law was changed in Holland to make it more difficult to buy dangerous poisons in shops. The policy of taking out life insurance on another person was also changed to make it more difficult and much more scrutinised. The Nederlandsche Panopticum wax museum in Amsterdam later added a figure of Maria Swanenburg to the Chamber of Horrors. She was certainly deadly enough to warrant her place in any waxworks of horror.

MARY ANN BRITLAND was born in 1847 in Bolton, Lancashire. In 1886, Mary purchased some poison because of an alleged rat problem at the rented house she shared with her husband and two daughters Elizabeth and Susannah. Well, you can probably guess where this tale is heading already can't you? Mary was a barmaid and factory worker. Life was pretty tough and money was tight. The poison she had purchased gave her a rather dark idea about how she might improve her modest financial circumstances.

Teenage daughter Elizabeth was the first to die by way of poison. Mary collected £10 in life insurance after the death of Elizabeth. Nothing suspicious about the death was noticed at the time - despite the fact that Elizabeth was nineteen and in previous good health. Mary Ann Britland murdered her 44 year-old husband next. This death was put down to epilepsy. Mary no doubt breathed a sigh of relief at this verdict and happily collected the life insurance.

Mary Ann Britland received a lot of sympathy as a result of this apparently tragic and random double loss she had suffered. A neighbour named Mary Dixon even invited Mary Ann Britland and her remaining daughter to come and stay with her. Unknown to

Mary Dixon though, Mary Ann Britland had designs on her husband Thomas Dixon and decided that her stash of rat poison should be deployed to get the wife out of the picture. Twenty-nine year-old Mary Dixon therefore became the third and, as it turned out, last victim of Mary Ann Britland.

By now though, Britland had pushed her luck as far as it would go. Three sudden deaths to those around her was simply too suspicious. An examination on the body of Mary Dixon found large quantities of poison and Mary Ann Britland was arrested. At her trial, Mary Ann Britland argued that she had only received modest sums for the deaths of her relatives so had no motive. Why would she kill her beloved daughter and husband for a pittance? That was Mary's argument and although it made the court think twice it didn't actually save her in the end. One thing that did contribute to sealing Mary's fate at the trial was various witnesses saying that there was no evidence of rats or mice at Mary's house and that they'd never seen her using rat poison to banish rodents. This obviously suggested she had another motive for purchasing the poison in the first place.

Mary Ann Britland was found guilty of murder and sentenced to death by hanging. Thomas Dixon, the husband of victim Mary Dixon, was acquitted of any participation of his wife's death at the trial. It transpired that Thomas Dixon had rebuffed the romantic advances from Britland and had no idea that she was planning to murder his wife. Mary Ann Britland was hung at Strangeways Prison on the 9th of August 1886. She wailed and screamed as she went to the gallows and insisted she was innocent. As she was about to be hung her hands got loose and she grabbed the rope in a desperate attempt to cheat death. Mary was then restrained by the wardens and the hanging went ahead as planned.

LOUISE VERMILYA was born in Cook County, Illinois in 1868. At the age of 16 she married a man named Fred - with whom she lived on near a farm. Fred died at the (then fairly advanced) age of 60 so at the time it wasn't deemed an especially suspicious death at all. He was presumed to have passed away as a consequence of heart trouble. Louise Vermilya received $5,000 as a result of her husband's death as she had made sure Fred had life insurance. Death though was soon to apparently follow Louise Vermilya around at a rate to rival Charles Bronson in the Death Wish movies.

Not long after Fred died, Vermilya's daughters Cora (who was eight) and Florence (who was four) both passed away. This was followed by the death of Lillian - the 26 year-old granddaughter of Fred. One of the genuinely odd things about Louise Vermilya around this time (and retrospectively it obviously makes more sense) is that the local undertaker later reported that she loved visiting the mortuary. Vermilya wasn't even employed there but she was always trying to find excuses to go to the mortuary and help out. She seemed to get a big kick out of death and being around dead bodies.

Louise got married again - this time to Charles Vermilya. Charles was dead within three years - leaving $1,000 to Louise. The next to bite the bullet was Harry Vermilyea - the step-son of Charles. Harry was said to have had a difficult relationship with Louise Vermilya and they argued a lot. Strangely though, all these deaths of people who had obvious connections to Louise Vermilya had yet to ring any alarm bells or attract any notable degree of scrutiny or suspicion.

In 1910 there was another death in the family when Frank Brinkamp, a son from Vermilya's marriage to Fred, passed away at the age of 23. Louise Vermilya picked up $1,200 when Frank died. Before he died, Frank told his wife that he was dying in a suspiciously similar fashion to his father. No prizes for guessing who had been killing all of these family members. By now Louise Vermilya had almost run out of relatives to murder and began to target people outside of her family. A man named Jason Ruppert died two days after dining with Louise. The next to die was a man named Richard Smith - who had rented a room from Louise and clearly made the unwitting mistake of eating food prepared by her. He lasted only two days after this fateful meal.

Some reports indicate that Smith married Louise despite the fact he was already married. His other wife expressed some suspicion after learning that her husband had suddenly passed away while with his new flame. Louise Vermilya was finally rumbled when a young police officer named Arthur Bisonette fell ill and died while renting rooms from her. His father had also dined at the house and reported experiencing dreadful stomach pains after the meal. He also recalled that he had seen Louise Vermilya sprinkling a white powder over the food before she served it. A police autopsy on the body of Arthur Bisonette revealed that he had been killed by arsenic. Further exhumations confirmed that Louise Vermilya was a serial poisoner.

There was a bizarre coda to the Louise Vermilya story because she then started poisoning herself in what presumed to be a suicide attempt. She became ill and attended court sessions in a wheelchair. It was then discovered that, before he died, Arthur Bisonette had been taking a medication that contained traces of arsenic. This made it more difficult to convict Louise Vermilya for that murder. The prosecution decided to try and convict her on one single charge of murder but they struggled to find enough medical evidence for a 100% cast iron case (despite the fact it was clearly no coincidence that all these people had died around Louise Vermilya).

Further complications ensued from the fact that it was difficult to find an impartial jury because there had been so much press coverage of the case. The prosecution wanted the option of the death penalty but this was impossible because male jurors were not comfortable with sentencing a woman to death - which called into question the likelihood of getting a guilty verdict. In the end the authorities decided a trial would be very expensive and have no guarantee of a conviction so they dropped all the (considerable) charges against Louise Vermilya and set her free! She didn't last much longer anyway, dying in 1913 at the age of 45. The odd and chilling thing about Louise Vermilya is that while the first murders had a financial motivation the later ones didn't. It seems that she simply enjoyed murdering people.

MARY ANN GEERING was born Mary ann Plumb in 1800. She is known as The Guestling Murderess. At the age of eighteen, Mary married a man named Richard Geering and they eventually lived in Guestling, Sussex. There were soon children in the marriage and Richard worked as a labourer. In 1846, Richard Geering was left £20 by a relative. That doesn't sound like much but it was a windfall to a cash strapped couple in that era.

Around this time Mary and Richard's oldest son became a widow and moved in with Richard and Mary. All three sons ended up at the cottage. In 1848, Richard Geering suddenly fell ill and died five days later. The cause of death was not deemed to be suspicious at the time. What was suspicious though was what happened next to the relatives who were all living in Mary's cottage. Twenty-one year-old George also fell ill with a mysterious but awful sickness and perished soon after. Then twenty-six year James was struck by identical symptoms and expired in similar fashion. The youngest of the sons, teenage Benjamin Geering, then fell ill in similar fashion.

The doctors who treated Benjamin decided to move him away from his mother and once they did this his condition began to improve and he eventually recovered. They of course noted this and came to an obvious conclusion. Mary Ann Geering had plainly been bumping off members of her own family. The bodies of Mary's relatives were exhumed and found to have ingested arsenic and opium. At the trial it was established the victims fell ill not long after eating food prepared by Mary. It was also established that Mary had purchased arsenic and poison despite having no rat problem in her house.

One of the most important pieces of evidence - and one that really sealed the fate of Mary - was that it was established that Mary Ann Geering had emptied the bank savings account of Richard Geering almost as soon as he had died. It seemed fairly evident that a financial motive for these murders was apparent. Mary confessed to the murders in the end and was sentenced to death by hanging. Her surviving son Benjamin testified against her at the trial.

Mary is said to have shown remorse for her crimes and did not try to pretend she was innocent. Mary Ann Geering was executed by hanging at Lewes on August the 21st, 1849. She was 49 years-old. The London times reported (as if it was the FA Cup Final or something!) that there was a rather disappointing turn out for Mary's hanging with only about 3,000 people showing up to see her die. 'In about two minutes the necessary arrangements were completed,' wrote the Times, 'and the wretched criminal ceased to exist.'

SARAH DAZLEY was born in Potton, Bedfordshire in 1819. She was an attractive woman who never had any shortage of male admirers. At the age of nineteen she married a man named Simeon Mead and they later settled in the village of Tatlow in Cambridgeshire. The couple had a son in 1840 who they named Jonah. When he was only seven months old though, Jonah died rather suddenly. Not long after this, Simeon Mead also died after falling ill.

Sarah married again - this time to twenty-three year old William Dazley. The marriage was obstreperous though and William was said to have struck her during altercations and arguments. Sarah apparently told friends that she would kill any man who raised a hand to her and she was true to her word. William Dazley soon fell ill with violent stomach cramps. He was then given pills by the doctor and seemed to be recovering. Ann Mead, the teenage daughter of Sarah's late husband, was also living there and helping out.

At some point though Sarah Cazley told friends that she was not happy with the treatment her poorly husband was receiving so was going to get some new medicine. She claimed she would get something from the village but in reality was just planning to make up her own batch of deadly pills. No prizes for guessing what happened when William started taking the pills supplied by his wife. He soon expired. There was no post-mortem because in those days people didn't tend to live for very long anyway.

Sarah took up with a new man at this point but he broke off the engagement when his friends and relatives told him about Sarah Dazley's history. They told him how her son, husband, and second husband had all suddenly fallen ill and then died. That was, they felt, all more than a little on the suspicious side. It was an open secret that more and more people thought that Sarah had bumped them all off. These whispers obviously reached those with authority and the Bedfordshire coroner ordered the exhumation of Sarah's second husband William to test this theory.

The whispers turned out to be true. William had died of arsenic poisoning. Sarah fled to London but was arrested there and brought back home for a trial. Sarah's defence was certainly creative. She claimed that her second husband William had murdered her first husband and son so they would be out of the picture and he could have her all to himself. Sarah said when she found out about this she killed William in revenge. To the surprise of no one, this defence did not fly very far in court and no one believed it. A jury didn't take very long to find Sarah guilty.

Although she was not charged with the murder of her infant son the judge commented at the trial that Sarah must be heartless indeed to kill her own child. It seemed fairly obvious that Sarah Dazley had killed all three of the relatives. Sarah Dazley was hung on the 5th of August 1843 outside Bedford Gaol. A crowd of about 10,000 turned up to watch. Legend has it that one of the interested spectators was the man who had (wisely in hindsight) broken off his engagement to Sarah. The strange thing about the case of Sarah Dazley is that there was no evidence she was impoverished or in debt. Money was not a salient motive in these murders. It seems as if Sarah just wanted to get rid of her husbands (and son) so she could constantly move onto a new man.

MARIE ALEXANDER BECKER was born in 1877 in Waasmont, Landen, Belgium. When she was a young woman she got a job in a sewing shop and began what seemed to be a happy and successful life. She eventually worked at a large fashion store on Pot d'Or Street in Liège and in 1906 married a man named Charles Becker Sr who had two sons. Behind the scenes though she wasn't happy. She found her husband dull and didn't get on with his relatives.

Marie eventually began to feel that life had passed her by and decided she wanted to make up for lost time. She eventually began an affair with a man named Lambert Beyer and poisoned her husband Charles with digitalis (a drug used for heart diseases). She then poisoned her lover too. Marie was clearly having something of a mid-life crisis because she took to visiting nightclubs and gathered a collection of young lovers (most of whom she had to bribe to share her bed). This all cost money and so she boosted her income by murdering the elderly patrons of her dress shop. She would slip the poison in a cup of tea and then when it began to take effect would take the victim home so they died in their house rather than her shop. This obviously made the deaths far less suspicious.

Marie is thought to have carried out at least eleven murders but many crime experts believe she probably murdered more people than this. She was a financially motivated serial killer. Marie simply wanted money to maintain her lifestyle and was perfectly willing to kill people if that was the only way to do this. She would only manage though to get hold of a minor sum of money from each victim. It wasn't exactly a rapid get rich scheme. Marie would even attend the funerals of many of her victims and was a convincing actress by all accounts, seeming suitably distraught at the graves.

However, once the funeral was over Becker would soon be back in a bar or nightclub looking as if she didn't have a care in the world. She would mock her victims and make jokes about them in private. Marie Alexandrine Becker was plainly not someone who was ever burdened by human emotions like guilt or remorse. Her killing spree came to an end when one of Marie's friends told her she was in an unhappy marriage. Marie told her friend that she should poison her husband and offered to supply the poison. The friend was rather disturbed by this and went to the police.

Marie Alexandrine Becker was found to have in her possession a bottle of poison and clothes and jewelry belonging to her elderly victims. Exhumations confirmed that a number of victims had died by poisoning. Marie insisted she was innocent and said the digitalis was for personal use but this was all complete nonsense. There was simply too much evidence against her. She was found guilty of eleven murders, five attempted murders, theft and forgery. The sentence was execution but this was commuted to life in prison. Marie Alexandrine Becker died in prison in Nazi occupied Belgium in 1942. She was 62 years old.

DAISY DE MAKER was a South African woman who gained notoriety in the early 20th century for being a serial killer. She was born Daisy Hancorn on 1 June 1886 in Seven Fountains, near Grahamstown, South Africa. De Melker was convicted for the murders of her two husbands and her only son. De Melker's first known victim was her husband, William Alfred Cowle. He died in 1903 under suspicious circumstances after ingesting arsenic.

In 1913, de Melker married her second husband, Robert Sproat. It probably won't come as a tremendous surprise to know that this marriage did not last for very long. Robert Sproat died mysteriously soon after their marriage. It was later discovered that he too had been poisoned with arsenic. Following the death of her second husband, de Melker collected a substantial life insurance payout. In 1923, she married her third husband, Sydney Clarence de Melker, who met a similar fate as the previous two. He fell ill and died in 1927, again due to arsenic poisoning.

After suspicion arose surrounding the deaths of her two husbands, an investigation was launched and de Melker was arrested in 1932. During the trial, it was revealed that she had administered poisonous doses of arsenic to her victims. Additionally, it was discovered that she had attempted to poison her daughter, who fortunately survived. Daisy de Melker was found guilty and sentenced to death. On 30 December 1932, she was executed by hanging at Pretoria Central Prison in South Africa. The case of Daisy de Melker remains one of the most infamous criminal trials in South African history. It highlighted the dark and disturbing actions of a heartless woman who took the lives of those closest to her simply for personal gain.

DELLA SORENSON was born in 1897. Between 1918 and 1923, Sorenson killed several people - all of whom were related to her. The murders took place in Howard County, Nebraska.
Sorenson was only in her twenties when her crimes came to light. Della Sorenson was another of those infamous poisoners. All of her victims were poisoned. The first victim was her one-year-old niece, Viola Cooper, in 1918. Sorenson said she killed this child as revenge because she'd fallen out with Viola's mother. That gives you some idea of Sorenson's mental state. She was willing to murder someone's child just because she'd had an argument with them.

Two years later Sorenson murdered her own husband and then killed her mother-in-law. Sorenson is also believed to have murdered three of her own children and attempted (unsuccessfully) to murder two others. When she attempted to kill her second husband, Della Sorenson finally attracted the sort of suspicion and scrutiny one might expect and she was arrested in 1925. Once in custody she confessed to the murders.

The most bewildering part of this crime is that no real motivation for the deaths was readily apparent. It's not as if Sorenson made any money by killing all of these relatives. Della Sorenson simply said that she enjoyed killing and always felt a surge of elation and happiness after she had poisoned someone to death. She never expressed any remorse for her crimes at all. The gravity of what she had done didn't seem to register at all for Della Sorenson. She just didn't care.

The chilling thing about this case was the way Sorenson would give trivial reasons for why she had killed. She said she murdered one child after it kept crying. She wafted away the murder of a husband by saying they'd had an argument. She even said that she killed people because she enjoyed a good funeral. "I like to attend funerals," she told the police. "I'm happy when someone is dying."

All of the murders took place in Sorenson's modest home. The relatives clearly detected no danger from her at all and trusted her.

Della, in her own warped imagination, seemed to think that these relatives had somehow deserved their tragic deaths. Sorenson was apparently rumbled when she gave two child relatives strychnine-laced candy but they managed to survive. She was deemed schizophrenic and sent to the state mental asylum. Della Sorenson was clearly a very troubled woman and it came as no surprise that the authorities deemed her to be too mentally unsound for a trial. She died in 1941.

LYDA SOUTHARD was born in Keytesville, Missouri in 1892. She had six husbands in all and killed four of them. As if that wasn't bad enough she also killed her daughter amd brother in law. You probably won't be surprised to learn that Lyda is commonly known as The Black Widow in true crime circles. Her first husband was Robert C. Dooley. The couple had a daughter together named Lorraine. Tragedy seemed to quickly surround Lyda though. Her daughter, husband, and her husband's brother all died in fairly quick succession.

Lyda explained away the death of her daughter by saying the child had drunk water from a polluted well. That was a blatant lie but it seemed to fool everyone at the time. Her husband's death was judged to have been from ptomaine poisoning and her brother in law was presumed to have been a victim of typhoid. Because people often died a lot younger in this era than they do today and medical science was far less sophisticated, poisoners like Lyda Southard were able to get away their crimes for longer than you'd imagine. If someone suddenly dropped dead of mysteriously fell ill in the early part of the 20th century it wasn't necessarily deemed to be suspicious.

A year or so later, Lyda married a man named William G. McHaffle but he died not very long into the marriage at all. In 1919 she married another man - this time Harlan Lewis. Within short three months of the couple getting hitched, Harlan Lewis was dead. Lyda then moved to Idaho and married a man named Edward Meyer. This marriage lasted a grand total of one month before Meyer dropped dead! As you might expect and hope, Lyda had by now finally started to attract suspicion concerning her remarkably bad misfortune when it came to husbands and relatives dropping dead at the drop of a hat.

An investigation into Edward Meyer's death established that arsenic had been responsible for his swift demise. Remarkably, while the authorities were trying to find Lyda Southard, she actually got married again. This was to Paul Southard (from whom she got her most commonly used name). Lyda tried to persuade Paul Southard to take out life insurance but he refused because he was in the army and already had this covered. At this point, Lyda was finally captured and given a ten-years-to-life sentence in the Old Idaho State Penitentiary.

Incredibly, Lyda Southard escaped from prison in 1931 and actually got married again while on the run! When she apprehended, Lyda served another eleven years in prison before earning parole. She died of a heart attack in 1958 in Salt Lake City, Utah. Lyda Southard was 65 at the time of her death. She is generally credited with six victims but it seems safe to assume that Lyda probably tried (and certainly planned) to kill a lot more people than that.

LYDIA SHERMAN was born Lydia Danbury in Burlington, New Jersey in 1824. Lydia was yet another of those female poisoner serial killers. She was an orphan as a child and (as was custom at the time) got married when she was only a teenager. Her husband was a man named Edward Struck and the couple soon had children. In the 1860s, Lydia, obviously tired of family life, decided to take out some life insurance on her husband. She then went and purchased some rat poison. When her husband died as a result of poisoning, no one suspected a thing so Lydia took out insurance on her six children and killed them too.

In 1868, Lydia married a farmer named Dennis Hurlbrut. Dennis was said to be in quite poor health and on his last legs but Lydia was clearly not a patient woman because she poisoned him too. In April 1870, Lydia took a job as housekeeper to Nelson Sherman (from whom she got her name). Sherman had a baby son and teenage daughter. Lydia became a trusted part of this family (Nelson Sherman even planned to marry her) and then - once she had lulled them into a false sense of security - poisoned them all.

Nelson himself was dispatched by means of rat poison in a mug of hot chocolate. By now though, Lydia had pushed her luck as far as it would go. A local doctor found these deaths highly suspicious and conducted an investigation. Sure enough, arsenic was found in the bodies and Lydia was arrested. Lydia Sherman surprised people in court as she was a very prim and proper looking woman who seemed an unlikely serial killer. She was of fairly low intelligence though and couldn't read or write.

Lydia Sherman's defence tried to argue that she hadn't meant to kill these people and that Nelson Sherman might have taken his life because he was heartbroken at the death of his children. This defence didn't stand up to much scrutiny and Lydia Sherman was sentenced to life in prison for her heartless crimes. She was a remarkably cold and ruthless killer in the way that she had no qualms about targeting children. After her conviction she dictated a confession - which perhaps suggested she did have some flickers of humanity and remorse.

Lydia actually escaped from prison and made her way to Providence, Rhode Island. She was soon captured though and died in prison several weeks later. In true crime circles, Lydia Sherman has attracted a number of sobriquets that include The Modern Lucretia Borgia, The Poison Fiend, The Borgia of Connecticut and The Queen Poisoner. Lydia Sherman died of cancer in 1878 at the age of 53. She was an exceptionally dangerous and calculating poisoner. No one was safe at all if they shared a house with Lydia Sherman. She is believed to have killed twelve people in all though some sources put the figure at ten. The real number of victims, as is often the case with serial killers, is difficult to verify for sure.

AMY ARCHER GILLIGAN was born in Milton, Connecticut, in 1873. She was one of ten children and got married to a man named James Archer in 1897. In 1901 the couple became caretakers and were hired to look after a widower named John Seymour. Seymour died in 1904 and (after arranging rent with the Seymour estate) they converted his home into a boarding house for the elderly. The house was known as Sister Amy's Nursing Home for the Elderly. James Archer died in 1910. Amy had (rather suspiciously) taken out life insurance on him a few weeks before but he was in pretty poor health anyway so there didn't seem to be anything too dodgy about his demise.

In 1913, Amy married Michael W. Gilligan. However, he died only three months into the marriage and left his entire estate to Amy. Highly suspicious wouldn't you say? His death was classified as an attack of acid indigestion. It later transpired that Amy had forged his will so that he left his money to her rather than his sons. Around 1916, Amy Archer-Gilligan was now known as Sister Amy in her nursing home for the elderly. She was a veritable Saint in the community. It was all a sham though - as was about to be revealed.

A man at the home named Franklin Andrews dropped dead one day while in the garden. His family were rather puzzled by this because he had seemed to be in excellent health. The family of the deceased man decided to investigate the home and do some detective work. They learned that Amy Archer-Gilligan had taken a $500 loan from Andrews just before he dropped dead. These findings were passed onto the authorities. It was the local newspaper though that took the most interest in the case.

The local newspaper learned that over fifty people had died in suspicious circumstances while in the care of Sister Amy. They also learned of the fact that Amy's two husbands had both died and left all of their money to her. As if that wasn't enough they also heard that Army often purchased large quantities of arsenic because she said she had a rat problem. When the newspaper (The Hartford Courant) began running stories about what they'd discovered, the authorities finally took action against Amy Archer-Gilligan.

It took a year to investigate the case but exhumations proved that Amy had been poisoning many of the tenants of her home to steal their money. It was also proven that Amy had poisoned her second husband. It took a jury only four hours to convict her. The death penalty was ruled out because she was deemed to be insane. Amy Archer-Gilligan was sent to a mental hospital in Middletown. She remained in this hospital until her death in 1962 at the age of 88. Though convicted of five counts of murder, Amy Archer-Gilligan almost certainly killed a lot more people than that.

TILLIE KLIMEK was born Teofila Gburek on October the 22nd, 1877 in Poland. Her family moved to the United States when she was an infant. In 1914 she got married and her husband died in 1914 after a sudden illness. Her second husband died soon after - as a did a lover who had given her the elbow. Tillie's third husband was a man named

Frank Kupczyk. Frank died in 1921. The odd and suspicious thing about this death at the time was that Tillie seemed to anticipate it was going to happen. Legend has it that Tillie even purchased a coffin before Frank had passed away.

Husband number four for Tillie was Joseph Klimek. However, when Klimek fell ill the doctors who treated him became suspicious and decided to run some tests. Sure enough, the medical findings reported arsenic poisoning. Tillie's cousin Nellie Koulik was also arrested because she was alleged to have supplied the poison and been an accomplice. Exhumations confirmed that Tille's previous husbands had all been poisoned. The investigation which followed discovered that neighbours and other relatives of Tillie had fallen ill or died after consuming food or drinks prepared by her.

Tillie was sentenced to life in prison while Nellie got a year behind bars. Tillie died in 1936 at the age of 60. The media at the time reported that Tillie was a psychic who predicted when her victims were going to die. This wasn't really true and more of a speculative embellishment than anything. It was probably a result of Tillie buying a coffin for her husband Frank before he died. This was hardly evidence of being a psychic. She had poisoned him so she knew full well he was going to die soon!

We don't know how many people Tillie Klimek killed for sure. Although she was only convicted of one murder, prosecutors at the trial apparently amassed enough evidence to plausibly connect Tillie to twenty suspicious deaths. Tillie Klimek made no effort to feign innocence or deny that she'd killed anyone. When asked if she'd murdered members of family at the trial she simply shrugged and admitted it as if it was all no big deal. The motivation for the murders is believed to have been (no surprise here) money. Tillie always tried to make sure her husbands had life insurance policies before she slipped them the dreaded arsenic.

BERTHA GIFFORD was born in Morse Mill, Missouri in 1871. She was one of ten children and twice married. Bertha was said to be a beautiful woman in her youth and eventually moved to Catawissa, Franklin County, Missouri. Here she became something of a local legend for her community spirit. Bertha would cook for neighbours and was an excellent chef. If anyone got ill or was feeling under the weather she would selflessly rush to their aid and care for them. In this capacity she even donned a nurses uniform - despite the fact that she wasn't a trained nurse and had no medical qualifications. This didn't stop her though from dispensing medical wisdom and her own solutions to ailments.

There was one other thing about Bertha that the locals seemed to appreciate. She never missed a local funeral. There were few things in life that Bertha loved more than a good funeral. Well, you can probably hazard guess where this story is heading. Naturally, it was none other than Bertha Gifford who was sending all these locals to the graveyard in the first place. In her duties as a 'nurse' and cook she was poisoning all and sundry. It didn't seem to make much difference to Bertha who she killed. She poisoned children and even her own mother in law.

One rather suspicious thing about Bertha, that maybe should have been picked up sooner, was the fact that she sometimes seemed to be visibly irritated and disappointed if one of her 'patients' made a recovery. That, in hindsight, was beyond suspicious. Bertha's tally of victims is impossible to verify for sure but most true crime accounts of her case put the number at seventeen (and this is at the very least). It later transpired that Bertha had a large stash of arsenic at her home because of an alleged rat problem. We obviously know now what she was really using this arsenic for and it had nothing to do with rats.

If someone died under her care (and this obviously happened an awful lot), Bertha would usually say that the victim had died of what she called gastritis. Bertha would always pretend to be some sort of medical expert and, surprisingly, this even seemed to fool genuine doctors for a time. Bertha was finally arrested in 1928 in relation to five suspicious deaths of people she had been caring for. The authorities suspected she had a hand in at least twelve other suspicious deaths in the area but proving this turned out to be very difficult. Bertha's trial only lasted for four days. She was judged to be completely insane and sent to the Missouri State Psychiatric Hospital where she died in 1951 at the age of 79.

ANNA MARIE HAHN was born Anna Marie Filse in Bavaria, Germany, in 1906. When she was still a teenager, Hahn had a child and claimed the father was a respected doctor. However, this respected doctor did not exist. It was something Hahn had made up to mitigate the stigma of being a single mother. Hahn's pregnancy with no marriage or husband was something of a scandal in the family and she was sent away to the United States in 1929. Anna Marie Hahn's family was fairly rich and conservative so you could say that they rather sent her into exile. She had become the black sheep of the clan.

Anna Marie ended up in Cincinnati, Ohio where she married a fellow German immigrant named Philip Hahn. They started a family together. Anna Marie is said to have briefly run a bakery but clearly didn't enjoy this much and it didn't last very long. Accounts of her life often say she had a number of gambling debts. One thing was certain in the end. Anna Marie Hahn liked money and would do literally anything to get her hands on it.

Alarm bells regarding the activities of Anna Marie first began to ring when she seemed unusually insistent that her husband should take out life insurance - despite the fact that he was quite young. Sure enough, her husband soon fell ill and was carted off to hospital (where he managed to survive) by relatives. With her marriage in tatters, Anna Marie took up a position caring for elderly men in Cincinnati's German community. You can probably guess what happened next. That's right. The elderly patients she was caring for soon began to suddenly and mysteriously die.

Anna Marie would borrow money from her patients before they died. One patient even left her a house in his will. She would earn their trust (and in some cases it seems even they love) before she poisoned them. The last victim was George Obendoerfer in 1937. Anna Marie plundered his bank account after she'd killed him. The police got suspicious of Anna Marie because of the bank transfer she had arranged so soon after the death of Obendoerfer. His body was found to contain poison - as were the bodies of her previous two patients after exhumations.

It transpired that Hahn was creative in her methods and used different poisons (including arsenic and croton oil) on different victims. A search of her home found a large stash of poison (in addition to belongings she had stolen from her victims) and she was taken into custody. After a four week trial, Anna Marie was sentenced to death. This came as a big shock to her. Anna Marie Hahn had been so confident of a not guilty verdict that she had her bags packed so that she was ready to go home. At the trial Anna Marie Hahn was cogent and well dressed and insisted she was innocent. The evidence though said otherwise.

As her execution loomed, Anna Marie became confessional and composed a written statement. 'God above will tell me what made me do these terrible things,' she wrote. 'I couldn't have been in my right mind when I did them. I loved all people so much. Now I am so close to death. Death is all around me. I have been here (on death row) for what seems another lifetime already. Several other people in this place have been called out. I hope that God will take care of my son, for I would not want anything to happen to my boy. I feel that God has shown me my wrongs in life and my only regret is that I have not the power to undo the trouble and heartache that I have caused.' Anna Marie Hahn was executed by electrocution at the Ohio Penitentiary on December the 7th, 1938. Her son Oskar was given a new identity and served in the United States Navy during World War 2.

ROBERTA ELDER was a Georgia serial killer who is believed to have poisoned at least fourteen people. She is believed to have killed for the first time in 1938. Her first victim was her husband John Woodward. Six months later, Roberta Elder's son from a previous also died at the age of thirteen. The victim count escalated from here on in. Elder killed more husbands, more children, and even a grandchild. It was only in 1952 that anyone began to suspect that something was suspicious about this family.

Rev. William H. Elder, who was the latest husband of Roberta Elder, fell ill after eating his packed lunch on a construction site. The doctor was called for and he had time to examine Rev. William H. Elder before the man passed away from what seemed to be a severe stomach complaint. The doctor became suspicious because the reddish tinge in the skin of the dying victim reminded him of a tinge in the skin of two Elder family children who had previously passed away. The doctor decided to bring in a coroner - who decided to do a test for arsenic. When this proved positive, exhumations on deceased Elder relatives took place and also found evidence of arsenic. It probably didn't come as a huge shock to learn that Roberta Elder was the financial beneficiary of these deaths when it came to life insurance.

It later transpired that were cases of Roberta arranging life insurance on relatives only weeks before they died. Like other notorious poisoners, Roberta Elder always made sure that she was the one tasked with looking after a family member when they fell ill. Roberta was arrested on suspicion of murder. She ludicrously claimed that she'd never heard of arsenic and knew nothing about poisoning but this was clearly not the case. Indeed, it was later established that she got hold of the poison from her brother's farm. Roberta Elder was found guilty of murder and sentenced to life in prison. She had literally killed everyone in her family.

No one was safe from Roberta Elder. She even killed little kids. And yet, despite her crimes there is very little information about Roberta Elder and her exploits. She is far less famous than other female serial killers (even ones who killed less people). This is felt to be because Roberta Elder was black and her victims were black. At the time this case was not deemed worthy of as much ink as a case involving white victims would receive. Sad but true, it seems that this case would be much more famous today if Elder and her victims had been white.

'Though Roberta Elder's victims died decades ago,' wrote aaihs.org, 'the phenomenon of consistently devaluing Black violent crime victims remains to this day, evidenced by the persistent public fascination with Nannie Doss and her white victims, while Roberta Elder and the victims she is accused of killing remain forgotten. Between 1952 and 1954, the Black press followed Elder's case through the criminal justice system, while law enforcement found more potential victims to blame on Elder and the white press took little interest. Meanwhile, mainstream media became distracted by the Giggling Granny who continues to attract infamy as a notorious female serial killer. The danger in ignoring Black victims is not only in the devaluation of Black life, but also in ignoring systemic oppression that makes Black people more vulnerable to violent crime and less likely to receive justice.'

JANIE LOU GIBBS was born in Cordele, Georgia in 1932. The story of Gibbs is rather strange by any standards. She was a mother and wife who had been married for eighteen years and was a highly respected member of local church community. That all changed in the end though. In 1965, Janie Lou Gibbs had a surprising change of career when she became a serial killer poisoner. The first victim was her husband Marvin. She poisoned him and when he was in hospital she brought him in a batch of soup she'd made. Naturally, the soup contained more poison just to finish him off. Marvin's death was not deemed suspicious though and it was assumed by the medical staff that he'd passed away as a result of a liver condition he had.

Several months later, Gibbs killed her youngest son (also named Marvin) by poison. A few months after this she killed another son (who was a teenager) by poisoning him. Strangely, the deaths of her children did not make anyone suspect foul play at the time. Once again it was assumed that medical conditions had resulted in the deaths. It was rather odd though to say the least that Gibbs didn't attract suspicion much earlier. You'd have to be very unlucky to have a husband and two young sons pass away in a matter of months! That's not exactly normal.

What might have mitigated any potential suspicion was the fact that Gibbs donated the life insurance money she was picking up from these family deaths to the church. It wasn't as if she was hoarding up a fortune for herself from these apparent family tragedies. Janie Lou Gibbs now had one teenage son left named Robert. Robert was a young father to a baby named Raymond. Well, you probably don't need to be a master sleuth to guess what happened to Robert and Raymond. Janie Lou Gibbs poisoned both of them. The death of another teenage son and a healthy infant to boot was simply too suspicious to ignore.

The autopsy on Robert found large quantities of arsenic in his system. Exhumations of the husband and other sons of Janie Lou Gibbs also revealed arsenic. She had killed her entire family. It didn't come as a huge surprise that Janie Lou Gibbs was initially deemed unfit to stand trial. She was clearly completely insane. A later trial though gave her life in prison. The police found Gibbs to be a rather bewildering woman when they first arrested her. She rarely answered any questions and mostly just stared off into space in silence. Gibbs never explained why she killed her family. All she said was - "I don't question God's work. The Bible says they will get their reward; and I'm sure they will."

One possible theory for the murders was that Gibbs enjoyed the sympathy and attention she got from neighbours and the church each time she suffered another tragedy. She also enjoyed the fact that she was giving the church money in the form of the life insurance. Her religious beliefs were clearly some sort of factor in the murders but obviously it was the frazzled mental health of Gibbs more than anything that made her unfathomably murder her entire family. She later developed Parkinsons and was treated in humane fashion and released into the care of her sister in 1999. She died in 2010.

BLANCHE TAYLOR MOORE became known as the Black Widow (not exactly an original nickname!) for her chilling ability to poison those around her. Born on February 17, 1933, in Concord, North Carolina, Blanche Taylor seemed like an ordinary woman. She was married four times and had two children. However, behind her seemingly ordinary life lay a sinister secret. Moore had a penchant for poisoning those close to her. It is believed that she was responsible for the deaths of her first two husbands, James Taylor and Raymond Reid. Her killing spree didn't stop there. Over the years, she also poisoned her boyfriend, her father, and even her own mother.

Moore's modus operandi was to administer arsenic to her victims. Arsenic was her preferred weapon of choice. She would mix it into their food or drink, ensuring that the poison went undetected. It was only after a series of mysterious deaths in her wake that suspicion started to fall on Moore. The first major breakthrough in the case came when Moore's boyfriend, Raymond Reid, became deathly ill and was rushed to the hospital. Doctors were puzzled by his symptoms and decided to perform a thorough examination. Their findings were astounding. Reid's body contained high levels of arsenic, a clear indication of foul play. This discovery led the authorities to exhume the bodies of Moore's previous husbands, James Taylor and Raymond Reid, as well as her parents. The results were shocking – all of them had been poisoned with arsenic.

Arrested in 1989, Moore was charged with the murder of her

boyfriend, Raymond Reid. The subsequent investigation revealed that she had also collected large sums of money from insurance policies taken out on her deceased husbands and other family members. Authorities suspected that financial gain was one of her motives for murder. The trial that followed was a media sensation, with Moore's seemingly innocent demeanour and her deeply religious background adding to the intrigue.

Moore was eventually found guilty of first-degree murder and sentenced to death. However, her sentence was later commuted to life imprisonment without parole due to concerns about her mental health. Despite her conviction, Moore (like most convicted killers) maintained her innocence, claiming that she was a victim of a conspiracy. To this day, she remains incarcerated at North Carolina Correctional Institution for Women.

VELMA BARFIELD was born in South Carolina in 1932. She had a pretty awful childhood by most accounts and there were stories that her father sexually abused her. At the age of seventeen, Velma got married and eventually had two children. She worked at a factory but didn't last long and was on a battery of prescription drugs. Her marriage was increasingly fractious and in 1969 she took her children and left her husband Thomas Burke.

The family home suspiciously burned down at this time - with Thomas Burke (who had passed out) still inside at the time. Not long afterwards, Velma married a man named Jennings Barfield. Less than a year into the marriage though, Barfield died. The cause of death was believed at the time to be a result of heart problems. He was said to have been having a lot of arguments though with Velma before his swift and unexpected demise.

In 1974, Velma's mother died after experiencing severe and painful stomach pains. Velma was employed as a caretaker around this time but the two couples she was employed to care for also suddenly and mysteriously died. Their symptoms were identical to those of Velma's late mother. You didn't need to be Columbo to suspect that death seemed to follow Velma Barfield around a little too much not to be highly suspicious. By now, Velma had acquired a boyfriend named Rowland Stuart Taylor. You can probably guess what happened to him. Before he died, Taylor had deduced that Velma had been forging his cheques.

After the death of Rowland Stuart Taylor, the police received a secretive tip that they should investigate Velma Barfield. Taylor's body was exhumed and found to contain arsenic. When the bodies of others who had died in the proximity of Velma Barfield were examined they were also found to contain arsenic. Velma was arrested and confessed to four murders. She was convicted and sentenced to death - despite objections from psychiatric witnesses who felt she was not of sound mind.

Velma Barfield became a Christian in prison and her last few years were spent ministering to prisoners. She also apologised for her crimes. It was all to no avail though as Governor Jim Hunt refused to grant a pardon. She was killed by lethal injection in 1984. Barfield had one of the more basic last meal requests as far as condemned prisoners go. For her last meal she simply asked for some Coca-Cola and a bag of Cheez Doodles.

JUDY BEUNOANO was born Judias Welty in Quanah, Texas in 1943. Judy Buenoano was known as The Black Widow. She poisoned her husband, drowned her son, and tried to kill her lover with a bomb! Judy, as is so often the case with killers and serial murderers, had a fairly lousy childhood. She was put up for adoption and suffered abuse from both her stepmother and stepfather. At the tender age of fourteen she got a short prison sentence for attacking her step-parents. Judy Buenoano was obviously someone who could only be pushed so far.

Rather than go back to her adopted family (who she clearly despised), Judy chose to go to reform school when her criminal sentence had ended. She left at the age of sixteen and got a job as a nursing assistant in Roswell. She became a mother soon after to a son named Michael Schultz. In 1962 she married an air force officer named James Goodyear and had two more children. She also had a business venture in the form of the Conway Acres Child Care Center in Orlando. James Goodyear died in 1971 of a mysterious illness and Judy cashed in his three life insurance policies. No, nothing suspicious about that at all! She then engineered a house fire to get more insurance money.

Soon after, Judy got a new boyfriend named Bobby Joe Morris. The couple moved to Colorado in 1972 but not before another suspicious house fire occurred. In 1978, Bobby Joe Morris died of a mysterious illness and Judy collected a generous life insurance payout. Judy changed her name to Buenoano (Judy had gone by a battery of various names in the past) around this time and moved back to Pensacola. Judy's son Michael Buenoano had joined the army by this time but he then suffered from very poor health. Michael suffered from paraplegia and wore leg braces. There were signs that suggested someone might be poisoning him.

In 1980, Michael went on a canoe trip with Judy and his brother James. After the canoe got into trouble he was left to fend for himself and ended up drowning because his leg braces were essentially like weights and made him sink. Judy told the authorities it had all been a complete accident and promptly collected Michael's military insurance payout. Judi now opened a beauty salon in Gulf Breeze and began dating a businessman named John Gentry II. By now though, the authorities were starting to become more than a little suspicious of Judy Buenoano. They found it rather odd that Michael had had three life insurance policies taken out on him shortly before he died. They also found evidence that signatures on these policies might have been forged.

Judy Buenoano had told John Gentry a pack of lies about her past. She claimed to be a nurse from Florida. Judy also insisted that they take out life insurance policies on one another. Another thing that Judy insisted on was that that Gentry should should improve his health by taking some special vitamin tablets she recommended. When these tablets made him feel ill she said he should increase the dose. It was pretty obvious in hindsight that these special tablets of Judy were not vitamin pills at all.

In 1983, Judy upped the ante from poisoning and strange canoeing accidents when she put a bomb in Gentry's car! The police found out that Judy had been going around telling friends that Gentry had a terminal illness and would be dead soon. After a complicated investigation they managed to link Judy to the bomb in Gentry's car. The bodies of Michael Goodyear, James Goodyear, and Bobby Joe Morris were all exhumed and found to contain arsenic. In 1984, Buenoano was convicted for the murder of Michael and the attempted murder of Gentry. In 1985 she was convicted of the murder of James Goodyear. Judy Buenoano went to the electric chair in 1998. For her last meal, she chose asparagus, strawberries, broccoli, tomatoes, and hot tea.

CHAPTER FIVE - MEDICAL PROFESSIONAL POISONERS

A hospital is a place that affords a serial killer a number of advantages. They have access to various drugs and medications which can be used to kill people and because the patients in hospitals are administered drugs and medications all the time it can be made to look like an accident or a mistake. Killers who operate in the medical world have historically been quite difficult to actually unmask - though sadly a lot of this has to do with the cumbersome, complex and self-serving bureaucracy in place at hospitals. Medical serial killers are rare but true crime history is liberally sprinkled with them nonetheless.

On a similar theme, murderous private nurses and caregivers also have advantages - especially if those they are caring for are vulnerable and elderly. Those who have abused their positions as caregivers and medical professionals to poison patients have done so for a range of different motivations. For some it was financial (in that they stole from the patients they murdered - or even got them to change their wills) and for others it was a 'God complex' - in that they became addicted to the power they wielded over life and death. In this chapter we shall take a look at some of the infamous poisoners who have operated in these fields.

JANE TOPPAN was born in Boston in 1854. She was known as The Angel of Death. Toppan murdered at least 31 people with lethal injections in her duties as a nurse. Her parents were Irish immigrants and life was not exactly plain sailing for Jane Toppan as a child. Her mother died of tuberculosis and Jane Toppan's father was said to be so crazy that he once tried to sew up one of his eyelids. Jane Toppan was a bright girl though and entered medical school in 1885.

She was known as Jolly Jane to her colleagues because she was always laughing and smiling. Everyone seemed to like her. She worked at Cambridge Hospital in Massachusetts and developed a fondness for working with patients who were sick or elderly. Jane Toppan first attracted mild suspicion in her medical duties because she was completely obsessed with autopsies. She was absolutely fascinated with death and loved going to the morgue. Jane Toppan used her patients at the hospital to experiment with the drugs morphine and atropine. She would vary the doses to see what reaction occurred in the patient. Naturally, she created bogus medical charts for her patients to disguise what she was actually doing.

Jane Toppan is said to have got a sexual thrill from her murders. She said she even climbed into bed with one patient she had just killed. In 1889, she worked at the Massachusetts General Hospital and continued to murder patients with overdoses. However, her murders were not just confined to the medical world. In 1895 she killed her landlord by poisoning and also murdered his wife. Jane Toppan then killed her sister Elizabeth with strychnine. You didn't have to be in hospital to be at risk from Jane Toppan. She would murder people anywhere given half a chance.

In 1901, Jane Toppan was hired as a private nurse to look after an elderly man named Alden Davis. You can probably guess what happened next. Yes, she murdered this man. But she didn't stop there. She also murdered his sister and two daughters. The relatives of the victims were understandably suspicious of Jane Toppan after these tragic and sudden deaths. They arranged for a medical test on the youngest daughter and the tests concluded the reason for death was poison. After she was taken into custody, Jane Toppan confessed to many murders.

Toppan told the police that she was perfectly sane and always knew exactly what she was doing. She said to the police - "That is my ambition, to have killed more people — more helpless people — than any man or woman who has ever lived." Toppan told the police that she experienced a thrill from having absolute power over patients and enjoyed taking them to the brink of death and then reviving them - and so on. Despite her claim that she was perfectly sane, it was clearly obvious that Jane Toppan was not sane in the least. Jane Toppan was so disturbed she had even poisoned herself once to appear ill and attract sympathy from a prospective boyfriend.

We will never know exactly how many people she actually killed. By any standards, Jane Toppan was completely ruthless. She once poisoned her best friend so that she could have her friend's job as a matron. Jane Toppan would kill literally anyone given the chance. As for explanations for why this woman became a compulsive killer, Jane Toppan was once jilted at the alter when she was supposed to get married. This is speculated to have been one of the sources of her anger and mental instability. "If I had been a married woman, I probably would not have killed all of those people," she said. "I would have had my husband, my children and my home to take up my mind."

Jane Toppan was found not guilty of her crimes by reasons of insanity and committed for life in the Taunton Insane Hospital. She died in 1938 at the age of 84. There was a rather dark irony when Jane Toppan was sent to the Taunton Insane Hospital. At one point, she refused to eat anything at the hospital and complained that someone was trying to poison her!

ANTOINETTE SCIERI was an Italian woman who moved to France

with her family when she was very young. During the First World War she worked at a nursing station which cared for the wounded. Scieri was (like most serial killers it seems) a prolific thief in her early years and stole money and valuables from wounded soldiers. She would even forge letters to their relatives and get them to send her money. As the wounded soldiers were ill or barely awake she was able to get away with her rather heartless thefts and fraud for a time. She was jailed though in 1915 for stealing a soldier's paybook but released after a fairly short sentence. Suffice to say then, Scieri had a heart of stone. She would do literally anything to get her grubby mitts on money and with her lack of any moral compass this was a dangerous combination indeed.

Scieri got married after this stint in prison and had some children but the marriage didn't last long and she ended up living with a man named Joseph Rossignol. Joseph Rossignol was a violent drunk and so this relationship was stormy to say the least. In 1920 they moved to the south of France and Antoinette Scieri came up a new way to make money. She got some work caring for elderly people. As you might suspect, having a woman like Antoinette Scieri caring for elderly and vulnerable people was a recipe for disaster. The unfortunate elderly folk under her care soon began shuffling off this mortal coil.

When an elderly husband and wife died while being looked after by Scieri, it roused no suspicion though because of their advanced age. It wasn't just her patients who Scieri posed a danger to. She also poisoned her lover Joseph Rossignol to death around this time. Her next victims were two elderly sisters who she poisoned with coffee. One of the sisters found her coffee bitter though and secretly poured it away. The other sister died. This incident fanned the first flames of suspicion concerning Antoinette Scieri.

Her last victim was a woman named Madame Gouan-Criquet. After she died, Gouan-Criquet's husband was very suspicious of the fact that his wife's condition seemed to get markedly worse each time she was visited by Antoinette Scieri. When he looked under the bed of his wife he found a bottle of the herbicide pyralion. Antoinette

Scieri had finally been rumbled. The bodies of a number of people who had died after being 'cared' for by Scieri were exhumed and found to contain a herbicide. These of course included the body of Joseph Rossignol. Scieri had been poisoning people with the sort of stuff you use to kill weeds.

Antoinette Scieri desperately tried to pretend she was innocent and blamed the murders on a neighbour but this was all proven to be nonsense. She eventually confessed and was sentenced to death in 1926. The death sentence though was commuted to life in prison. The authorities deemed Scieri to be of sound mind and not insane. She knew exactly what she was doing when she was poisoning all those poor people and was a calm and calculating killer. She was released from prison in 1960 and died several years later. Antoinette Scieri was a classic example of a killer who dons the 'mask of sanity' and hides in plain sight. She was said to have an excellent bedside manner and those people who employed her thought she was kind and caring. They thought she was a really nice woman. Nothing could be further from the real truth.

JOHN BODKIN ADAMS was born in 1899 in Randalstown, Country Antrim. Whether or not he was serial killer is still open to question. He was suspected of murdering over a hundred of his patients for financial gain but was acquitted of the one charge of murder he did face. It could be that Adams was simply an advocate of assisted dying. It could also be though that he was the forerunner to Harold Shipman. The real truth was never really established. Adams was a doctor in the town of Eastbourne and had many elderly patients. It transpired that around 132 of these patients, shortly before their deaths, changed their will to include Dr Adams. That seems more than a little suspicious doesn't it?

Why would anyone suddenly change their will near the end of their life and leave money and valuables to their doctor? Wouldn't you want the money to go to your relatives instead? Your kids and grandchildren? John Bodkin Adams had attracted suspicion in Eastbourne because two of his deceased patients even left him a Rolls-Royce in their will.

There were certainly alarms about Adams. One family complained that their relative got worse because Adams kept injecting her with morphine. There were also accounts of how he was the wealthiest doctor in England and living a lavish lifestyle. Where was he getting all this money from? Well, from his patients it seems.

Adams was even accused of killing one patient with an overdose of sleeping pills. He was naturally then named in the will of this patient once they had expired. When a woman named Amy Ware died in his care, Adams said he was not a beneficiary in her will EVEN though he was. Why did he lie about this? Annabelle Kilgour died in 1950 after Adams gave her extra strong sedatives. In her will she left him £200 and a clock. Julia Bradnum, a patient of Adams, died in 1952 at the age of 85. Adams persuaded Bradnum to sell her house before she died and she also left him £600 in her will. Hilda Neil Miller, who was 85, died in 1952 while being treated by Adams. A relative of Hilda said she saw Adams rifling through Hilda's valuables and pocketing them after she died. Adams then quickly arranged the burial himself. There were countless suspicious incidents like this relating to Dr John Bodkin Adams.

The whispers and gossip surrounding Adams got so intense in the end that the police began investigating the wills of his patients and arrested him. They focused in particular on the death of Edith Alice Morrell. Morrell was a patient of Adams who died from a cocktail of heroin and morphine given to her by the doctor. Adams was left some money and a Rolls-Royce as a result of her death. Dr John Bodkin Adams, thanks to a rather shrewd QC, was cleared of charges of murder. What saved him was that the nurses looking after Morrell had been forced to concede that they kept detailed notes on her treatment. The nurses suspected Adams of foul play but nothing in their notes proved it. He was either innocent or very careful. Either way, the end result was that he was a free man and cleared of the alleged charges that he'd been bumping off old ladies after getting them to change their will.

The prosecution also failed to find any fellow doctors willing to argue that this was a clear case of murder. One strange thing that also went in favour of Dr John Bodkin Adams was the fact that he also managed to avoid having to give any evidence himself. He wasn't questioned in court. This was presumably a tactic by his defence team so they could avoid having him cross-examined by some clever barrister. After the trial, Adams was struck off the medical register for forging prescriptions. Amazingly though he was reinstated as a GP in 1961. Would you want to be treated by a doctor suspected of killing over a hundred of his patients? Adams later became President (and Honorary Medical Officer) of the British Clay Pigeon Shooting Association. He died in 1983. Though friends believed he was innocent the media and public always thought Adams was guilty. There was certainly a lot of evidence which suggested he was up to something dodgy but this evidence was clearly not strong enough to secure a conviction.

DOROTHY JEAN MATAJKE, born in 1930 and a resident of Nevada, murdered three people by poisoning in Arkansas in 1987. She is (predictably) now known as The Arkansas Poisoner. Matajke worked as a nurse's aide and cared for the elderly. Several of her patients died in suspicious circumstances but the authorities patently did not suspect foul play because she was only convicted of fraud and sentenced to five years in prison. Matajke was very lucky at the time she was only charged with fraud rather than investigated for murder. The authorities didn't seem to be aware of how serious her crimes really were. Matajke actually escaped from prison but was recaptured in 1980. When her sentence ended she went to Little Rock and (believe it or not) was somehow able to resume her old duties as a carer. Background checks were obviously not as stringent in those days.

In 1985 she moved in with Paul Kinsey and his wife Opal as their nurse. Paul was 72 and Opal was 71. Matajke was essentially a live in companion. Her duties were to fetch their groceries and prepare their meals and medication. She was also supposed to supply them with companionship and kindness but these two qualities were sorely lacking in the thoroughly heartless Dorothy Matajke. Opal Kinsey suspiciously died a few months after Matajke began her duties. The cause of death was assumed to be cancer. Paul Kinsey wasn't so sure though. He had noticed that the food and medication being served to him by Dorothy Matajke seemed to making him feel worse rather than better.

Kinsey (very sensibly) eventually stopped eating Matajke's food and declined her pills. He then (even more sensibly) fired Dorothy Matajke and booted her out of the house.

Matajke had another patient at this time though named Marion Doyle. Doyle was suffering from cancer and died only nine days after Dorothy Matajke started caring for her. At first the authorities thought Doyle might have taken her own life but the plot thickened when they looked into Marion Doyle's finances and saw that a number of cheques from Doyle had gone to Dorothy Matajke. The money ran into the thousands. The signature on the cheques was very suspicious and appeared to have been forged.

The body of Marion Doyle was therefore exhumed and found to contain traces of arsenic. By this time Paul Kinsey, who had also obviously already been poisoned by Dorothy Matajke, was almost on his death bed. The police searched the home of Dorothy Matajke and found arsenic. She was charged with first degree murder in the case of Doyle, and first degree battery in the case of Opal Kinsey. Kinsey subsequently died in 1987, so Matajke was charged with first degree murder for the poisoning of him too. In 1987 Matajke - aged 56 - was sentenced to life for killing Paul Kinsey and later sentenced to 60 years for killing Marion Doyle after a plea bargain. Dorothy Matajke was a very ruthless woman who preyed upon ill and elderly people purely for financial gain. She was just about the last person in the world you'd want caring for a relative.

HAROLD SHIPMAN was born in Nottingham in 1946. Shipman was a GP in Manchester who murdered (at least) 218 of his patients with injections of diamorphine (heroin) from 1975 to 1998. He was known as Doctor Death in the British media when his shocking secret came to light. Shipman trained at the Leeds School of Medicine and became a qualified doctor in 1970. He was married with children and loved the sport of rugby union. Harold Shipman seemed like the most normal person in the world. The chances of him one day becoming one of the most notorious serial killers in history must have seemed laughable at this stage of his life.

After working at a hospital, Shipman became a GP at a medical centre in Yorkshire. In 1975, Shipman was found to be addicted to a pain reliever called Pethidine (Demerol). He was forced to go to rehab for this addiction. Shipman then worked at the Donneybrook Medical Centre in Hyde, Manchester. Shipman appeared on the British documentary television show World in Action in 1982 talking about new treatments for the mentally ill - thus joining that select group of serial killers who appeared on television before their crimes came to light.

By the early 1990s, Shipman had three hundred patients at his practice and was a respected pillar of the local community. However, unknown to his patients and the community, Shipman was secretly killing his elderly patients by the dozen. Shipman first aroused suspicion in 1988 when a funeral home noted that he seemed to order a strangely high number of cremations. The police were called in but found no firm evidence of anything criminal or suspicious.

Shipman was caught in the end because he murdered an elderly woman who used to be the local Mayor. The woman's daughter was a lawyer and became very suspicious of Shipman. This suspicion was confirmed when she discovered that her late mother's will had been recently changed so that Shipman received the inheritance (which amounted to £386,000). The victim's daughter demanded that a medical examination of her late mother should take place to investigate evidence of foul play. The body was dug up and - sure enough - found to contain diamorphine. Dr Harold Shipman was naturally arrested.

People who knew Shipman were absolutely bewildered by the revelation he had been secretly killing his patients. They simply couldn't believe it. He was known by everyone to be a kind man who spent his spare time growing vegetables in his garden. No one had ever detected anything sinister or troubled about Harold Shipman at all. The body count is so high that we might never know just how many people Shipman killed. It is possible that Shipman's true kill count might be pushing 300.

And yet, Shipman never confessed to anything. He never admitted killing a patient (despite the overwhelming evidence against him) and never provided any explanation for why he had done these awful things. His wife stood by him too. Mrs Shipman maintained that her husband was innocent and supported him during the trial. Harold Shipman was convicted in 2000 on fifteen counts of murder but hung himself (using bed sheets) in prison in 2004. He was 57 years-old. Shipman was reading Henry IV by Shakespeare in his cell just before he committed suicide.

Shipman could not be buried for fear that his grave would be attacked. In the end he was secretly cremated with only his wife and children in attendance at the service. It remains a mystery why Harold Shipman did what he did but one theory pertains to the death of his mother from cancer when he was a boy. She required sedatives and regular medication to ease her pain. It is speculated that Shipman, who was clearly not the most mentally stable man, had an enduring obsession with putting people to 'rest' as had happened to his mother.

Another theory as regards the motivation of Shipman is (of course) financial. After Shipman was arrested, the police found that he had a large stash of jewelry he'd taken from victims and hidden in his garage. As a result of the Harold Shipman case, death certificate practices and the paperwork needed for a cremation in England were both reviewed and changed. The story of Harold Shipman remains very strange and unfathomable - not to mention very disturbing. True crime bios sometimes refer to him now as The Doctor Jekyll of Hyde. Harold Shipman truly was a bizarre and inexplicable killer.

MARIANNE NOLLE was born in 1938 in Cologne, North Rhine-Westphalia, Germany. Nölle is another in the long line of medical killers. To the world at large she was a competent and respected nurse but in reality she was killing patients with overdoses of Truxal. Chlorprothixene, sold under the brand name Truxal, is a sedative and antipsychotic. Overdose symptoms can be confusion, hypotension, and tachycardia. Nölle killed seven patients from 1984 to 1992 but she is believed to have attempted to kill around seventeen patients in all.

The oldest victim of Marianne Nölle was 91 years-old. None of the victims were terminally ill. Marianne Nölle would rob the victims after she killed them and take any money or valuables they had with them. Her heartless crimes eventually began to attract suspicion. A grandson of one of her victims started to become suspicious and scrutiny of Marianne Nölle became heightened as a consequence. With more relatives - and also a hospital supervisor becoming suspicious - exhumations took place which established that Nölle's patients had not died of natural causes at all. They had been hastened to their grave by this wicked medical killer.

Marianne Nölle was 57 years-old by the time of her trial. She sat silent through most of it and only spoke at the end to insist she was innocent. In 1993 she was sentenced to life in prison. Nölle, in a rare show of emotion, became tearful at this. The judge described Marianne Nölle as a very heartless and manipulative two faced woman. Her patients all loved her but little did they know she was only interested in killing them so that she could take what little money or valuables they might have.

Marianne Nölle never confessed to any of her crimes or provided any explanation for why she had killed these patients. The judge at the trial said she had taken it upon herself to play 'master' over life and death. Her guilt was never in question as four cans of Truxal were found in her apartment after she was arrested. The chilling thing about Marianne Nölle is that her patients all trusted her because she seemed so genuine and caring. Little did they know how dangerous she really was.

GENENE JONES Genene Jones was born in Texas in 1950. She was adopted as a child and worked as a beautician before deciding to go to nursing school. Jones also got married and had children of her own. She eventually worked as a licensed vocational nurse (LVN) at the Bexar County Hospital (now University Hospital of San Antonio) in the paediatric intensive care unit. However, an unusually large number of children seemed to die during her shifts. Jones would inject digoxin, heparin, and other drugs into patients to induce a medical emergency. She would then swoop in to revive them. Tragically a number of children because of this.

A motive for these murders was never established but Genene Jones, like all 'Angel of Death' medical killers, apparently developed a God complex. She was exhilarated by the power that she had over life and death and had become addicted to the practice of taking a child to the brink of death and then resuscitating them. Nurses who worked with her later recalled that Jones seemed to get strangely excited when a patient fell ill and even used to offer predictions on when the patient in question might expire.

It is impossible to say how many children she killed through her activities. Though she was convicted of two murders, fresh charges arrive to this day and a conservative estimate would put the number of victims around forty at the very least. The Bexar County Hospital was aware of the high number of deaths and feared a lawsuit so they simply dismissed all the licensed vocational nurses and replaced them with registered nurses. They also shredded medical records to protect themselves. The loss of these records later made prosecuting Genene Jones more complicated than it should have been. The conduct of this hospital was a scandal.

After the Bexar County Hospital dismissed their nurses, Genene Jones got a job at a pediatrician's clinic in Kerrville, Texas. Once again though she was soon up to her old tricks. A doctor there found a puncture in a bottle of succinylcholine which only Jones had access to out of all the nurses. Succinylcholine is a medication used to cause short-term paralysis as part of general anesthesia. People under the heavy influence of this drug can't breathe.

Chelsea McClellan, a baby at the clinic, had died after Jones gave her some shots. Jones is believed to have killed around six children at this clinic.

Jones tried to use an insanity defence as her trial loomed but this didn't wash. The prosecution proved that she was perfectly sane and knew exactly what she was doing when she killed those patients. In 1985, Jones was sentenced to 99 years in prison for killing 15-month-old Chelsea McClellan with succinylcholine. In the second trial (for another hospital), she received 60 years. Genene Jones was indicted on new charges in recent years - which ended any lingering hopes she might have had of parole or freedom one day. In 2020, Jones pleaded guilty to causing the death of an eleven month old bay who had been under her care in 1981.

MICHAEL SWANGO was born in 1954 in Tacoma, Washington. Swango was a good student, played the clarinet in a band, and joined the Marines when he left school. You might think this would be a good start in life and set him on the straight and narrow forever but, sadly, you'd be completely wrong about. Swango was, it seems, what you might justifiably call completely crazy. It is said that Swango's personality seemed to change when a girlfriend left him. As a consequence of this he became reclusive and abandoned college for the army. His father had been an officer in the army though so this was by no means an eccentric or strange career path to take.

Swango studied chemistry and biology at Quincy University after leaving the Marines although early clues about his character were retrospectively apparent here because he lied about his time in the army and claimed to have won various awards for bravery. In reality Swango had seen no combat at all during his time in the Marines. Swango then attended the Southern Illinois University School of Medicine - though his time here was difficult because his grades were poor and he began to display a rather morbid fascination with gruesome imagery and death. In his third year Swango began to spend more and more time with ill patients and several of these seemed to die in a manner that is suspicious today (now that we know of the true nature of Swango) but didn't attract any attention at the time.

Swango was hired as a surgical intern at the Ohio State University Medical Center in 1983 and then entered a neurosurgery residency. Swango soon attracted suspicion due to patients dying in his care but, in what would sadly be a recurring pattern, he was able to get away with his activities and keep working in medicine. One of the odd things about Swango is that he didn't simply target his patients but also poisoned co-workers. Swango was simply addicted to poisoning people and seemed fascinated by the effect it had. In this he had some similarities with the British killer Graham Young.

Swango became an emergency medical technician with the Adams County Ambulance Corps in Quincy but his colleagues soon deduced that whenever Swango gave them any food or drink to consume they fell ill thereafter. In 1985, Swango was convicted for poisoning co-workers and sentenced to five years in prison. Swango served four years of his sentence and then got as a job laboratory technician for ATICoal in Newport News. Well, you can probably guess what happened next. That's right. His work colleagues seemed to come down with a mysterious illness whenever they worked with Swango. He was up to his old arsenic themed tricks again.

Swango decided to make a sharp exit. What he desired more than anything was to get back into medicine but his criminal past obviously made this impossible. So he decided to change his name to Daniel J. Adams and even forged a document to pretend that his criminal offense had been a six month minor charge for nothing serious. Amazingly, Swango managed to secure a battery of medical jobs again in various places - where naturally he was up to his old tricks again and patients began dying dying in suspicious circumstances.

Swango eventually attracted the attention of investigative reporters and the American Medical Association. Swango also had a relationship with a nurse named Kristin Kinney - who later committed suicide. Kristin was found to have arsenic in her system when when she died. Her mother spoke out against Swango - joining the growing chorus against him. Swango must have realised by now that the net was tightening around him. He fled to Atlanta and got a job as a chemist but he was fired after the FBI (who were now also investigating Swango) warned his employer that Swango was a dangerous man suspected of many crimes relating to poison.

The old saying that truth is stranger than fiction certainly applies to Michael Swango because what he did next sounds like the plot of a far-fetched television thriller movie. Swango fled to Zimbabwe and got a job in a hospital! As you can probably imagine, patients at the hospital soon started to get sick. Swango even poisoned his landlady - which was a big mistake because this attracted the attention of local police. They quickly deduced that Swango was a dodgy character and got in touch with the FBI. Swango made a doomed attempt to flee to Saudi Arabia but he was arrested at Chicago-O'Hare International Airport.

Michael Swango was sentenced to three years for fraud but he knew a much more serious case against him for his medical crimes was being prepared and so accepted a plea deal. He was eventually sentenced to three consecutive life terms. It is believed that Swango may have killed as many as 60 people but - as ever in cases like this - the true figure could be much higher than that.

CHARLES EDMUND CULLEN was born in West Orange, New Jersey, in 1960. Cullen was a male nurse who was discovered to have deliberately given dozens of patients lethal overdoses in a number of hospitals. He is believed to have done this for the first time in 1988 but he was only convicted in 2008. Cullen apparently tried to commit suicide when he was nine years-old by drinking dangerous chemicals. When he grew-up he joined the United States Navy but attempted suicide again and had to spend some time in a psychiatric ward. After he left the navy, Cullen decided to take a nursing course and became qualified in 1986. He got married and found employment at a hospital.

Cullen left his first hospital because of an incident where he was found to be tampering with IV drips. He may have killed dozens of patients already though. His next post was at Warren Hospital in Phillipsburg. He killed three patients there by giving them too much heart medication. Once again, there were almost certainly more victims. The family of one of the elderly victims were very suspicious of the hospital and Cullen in particular. Members of staff had to take a lie detector test as part of an investigation. No action was taken in the end but Cullen had to move on anyway and leave the hospital.

Cullen came under suspicion in most of the hospitals he worked in but somehow managed to survive numerous investigations. Tragically, it is believed that the chronic shortage of nurses was the main reason why he kept being employed again. He continued to work in hospitals in the 1990s and also continued to kill patients. He later told prosecutors that he killed five patients in 1996 alone. While at St. Luke's Hospital in Bethlehem, Cullen killed five more patients and was the focus of an investigation that lasted nearly ten months. He was dismissed from the hospital but no criminal action was taken against him.

Cullen then got employment at the Somerset Medical Center in Somerville, New Jersey. He killed a dozen or more patients at this facility with digoxin, insulin, and epinephrine. The staff at the Somerset Medical Center became suspicious of Cullen because he often seemed to be in the rooms of patients that were not assigned to him. This feeling of suspicion was heightened when they noticed that he would sometimes ask for a medication that hadn't been prescribed to anyone under his care. More patients continued to die in suspicious circumstances and the police were called in. The police put Cullen under surveillance and made other nurses wear wire taps. They collected enough evidence to charge Cullen and he made a full confession.

Cullen told prosecutors that he had sought to mitigate the pain and suffering of patients but this evidence was thrown out because of the fact that many of these patients had no critical or terminal condition and would have recovered if he hadn't killed them. In 2006, Cullen was sentenced to eighteen consecutive life sentences in New Jersey. Prompted by the Cullen case, Pennsylvania, New Jersey, and 35 other states adopted new laws which encourage employers to give honest appraisals of workers' job performance and which give employers legal protections when they provide a truthful employee appraisal. It is not known exactly how many patients Cullen killed in the end but a conservative estimate is most likely over forty at the very least.

RICHARD ANGELO was born in Long Island in 1962. He was a model boy scout and a good student by all accounts. As a young man entered a two-year nursing program at Farmingdale State College and then worked at a number of medical facilities. Angelo became known as a nurse who was good during a crisis. Angelo even volunteered as an EMT with the fire department in his spare time. However, as his colleagues were soon to discover, it was usually Angelo who created the crisis in the first place. In 1987 he was accused of poisoning a patient at then Good Samaritan Medical Center in West Islip, Long Island by injecting Pavulon through his I.V. The elderly patient immediately became ill as a consequence.

Angelo had the been the night supervisor in a special unit full of vulnerable and elderly patients. This was a recipe for disaster to say the least because it gave him free access to a unit full of patients who had come to trust him - which turned out to be a big mistake. What had rumbled Angelo was the fact that one of the patients he had injected with a dangerous and paralysing cocktail of drugs had managed to press the assistance button before he succumbed to the effects of the drugs and this had made a nurse rush to the scene. The nurse decided to take a urine sample from the patient for tests. The tests were positive for the drugs Pavulon and Anectine - both of which were then found in Angelo's locker and house.

Angelo was arrested and the full catalogue of his wicked medical activities soon came to light. A number of dead patients were exhumed after Angelo confessed that this wasn't the first time he had done something like this. Angelo is believed to have poisoned over 30 patients - which resulted in at least ten deaths. Angelo said that his motivation was that he liked to play the 'hero' and bring a patient to the point of death and then save them. "I wanted to create a situation where I would cause the patient to have some respiratory distress or some problem, and through my intervention or suggested intervention or whatever, come out looking like I knew what I was doing. I had no confidence in myself. I felt very inadequate."

A number of medical killers have this psychology. They like to play God with the lives of their patients and become addicted to the power they wield over life and death. Angelo was initially well respected by his colleagues at the hospital because of his calmness and apparent dedication. However, the unusually high number of patient emergencies during his shift eventually began to attract suspicion.

In December 1989, Angelo was found guilty on two counts of murder, one count of manslaughter, and one count of criminally negligent homicide. Sadly, it is believed he may have killed more patients than his official tally indicates. On January 25, 1990, he was sentenced to 50-years-to-life in prison. Angelo was only 27 years-old at the time of his sentencing. Angelo's defence team had claimed in court that he suffered from a form of multiple personality disorder and didn't really know what he was doing. However this defence obviously proved futile in the end. The court was convinced that Angelo knew exactly what he was doing when he poisoned those patients.

DONALD HARVEY was born in Butler County, Ohio, in 1952. Harvey is another of those 'Angel of Death' medical killers. He claimed to have killed nearly 90 people in the end although the true number is almost impossible to ever know. It honestly wouldn't surprise you though if Harvey had killed close to a hundred people. Harvey dropped out of high school and didn't have the greatest education. As an adult he worked as an orderly at hospitals and this enabled him to kill dozens of patients. Many of his victims were cardiac patients. His first medical job was as an orderly at the Marymount Hospital in London, Kentucky. He said this is where he started killing.

Harvey was said to love going to the morgue in the hospital and always dispensed a lot of black humour about death to colleagues. His methods of murder were not limited to any one means. He turned off ventilators, used arsenic, suffocation, sabotaged catheters, and even injected people with hepatitis. Rather like Jane Toppan, his murders were not confined to hospitals either. He poisoned his roommate, his roommates father, and two neighbours. These actions completely contradicted his later claim that he had only done 'mercy' killings of sick patients. That was blatantly not true. Donald Harvey was perfectly capable of killing anyone anywhere.

Harvey was finally rumbled when an autopsy on a patient found large traces of cyanide. The police decided to investigate the staff at the hospital and they found out that Donald Harvey had once been dismissed from a hospital after he was caught stealing body parts. This, at the very least, made Harvey sound odd and suspicious. When the police questioned Harvey he confessed to giving the patient cyanide and claimed to have killed dozens of people. Subsequent investigations into suspicious deaths at the hospitals he had been employed in showed that he was probably wasn't lying.

As for how he got away with his crimes for so long, Donald Harvey later said - "Most of the doctors would be so overworked, so busy, that a patient could die and the family doctor would not come in and pronounce the person dead. They'd have a resident do that. They just pronounce him dead and send him straight to his funeral home. The doctors go and spend all these years in school. And they'd always come in with this kind of - superior attitude. You know, 'I know everything.' But yet, they didn't know nothing." Harvey said he enjoyed the power and control that the murders gave him.

Donald Harvey agreed to confess to as many murders as he could remember (with names and dates of course) as part a bargain to avoid the death penalty. In 1987, Harvey plead guilty to 24 counts of first-degree murder. In accordance with the plea agreement, he was sentenced to three concurrent terms of life in prison. Harvey's lawyer later wrote that Harvey told him he used to light a candle, put it on top of a skull, and then draw up a list of people in the hospital he was going to kill. Donald Harvey was simply obsessed with killing people. In 2017, Donald Harvey was found beaten to death in his prison cell. He was 64 years-old.

VICKIE DAWN JACKSON was born in 1966. In 2006 she pleaded no contest to charges that she had murdered ten patients at Nocona General Hospital in Texas. Jackson worked as a vocational nurse at the hospital and would use an overdose of Mivacron (a muscle relaxant) to kill the patients. Jackson had always wanted to be a nurse and worked hard to pass her exams. However her daughter later said that Vickie Dawn Jackson was always a strange and unpredictable woman prone to rages. She didn't seem surprised at all to learn that her mother had been killing patients.

The hospital Jackson worked in was very small and so the workers there were on intimate terms with their patients. Over the course of 2000 and 2001, twenty patients died on the ward during the night shifts covered by Jackson. In that same time frame, not a single patient died during the night shifts not covered by Jackson. A lot of these patients were in the hospital for very minor conditions or injuries so the deaths were obviously suspicious to say the least.

In 2002 it was discovered that twenty bottles of Mivacurium had gone missing at the hospital. Syringes with traces of this drug were found in Jackson's trash. Exhumations of the patients who had died then revealed Mivacurium overdoses as the cause of death. The hospital had been subject to a negligence lawsuit from relatives of those that had died there in the past but Jackson kept working throughout this time.

What was especially chilling about Jackson's activities is that she targeted a number of people who she thought had slighted her. She tried to kill one patient who had called her fat and also killed her estranged husband's grandfather. The motivation for some these murders was tragically petty to say the least. Jackson was arrested in 2002. After a mistrial (caused by a prosecutor's comments) she pleaded no contest in 2006. Jackson received life in prison for ten murders.

Not all of Vickie Dawn Jackson's victims were named due to privacy laws. Jackson clearly killed many more than ten patients but identifying how many is very complicated. Vickie Dawn Jackson never admitted any guilt and never offered any explanation as to why she killed these patients. It is believed that she plead no contest because her daughter was going to testify against her and say she was a dreadful mother. Vickie Dawn Jackson knew that she was going to be convicted whatever happened at the trial so she simply decided to cut to the chase and avoid the trial altogether.

ELIZABETH WETTLAUFER was born on Ontario, Canada in 1967. She studied nursing as a young woman and was eventually employed in a care home. Her time at Caressant Care though was plagued by problems related to her drug and alcohol addictions. She was eventually fired for various infractions - which included getting medications mixed up and being found passed out drunk in a storeroom. Wettlaufer was then employed at the Meadow Park Care Center but her time there was cut short when she had to have treatment for her drug problems.

After this Wettlaufer had a battery of medical positions in different places but - once again - never lasted very long. She was caught stealing from one care home and her habit of turning up for work drunk or high meant she was not a very reliable employee to say the least. The last thing a medical business (not to mention the patients) needs is the nurses turning up to work drunk or high on drugs. This was only the tip of the iceberg though. Turning up for work drunk or stealing was one thing but Wettlaufer was also trying to kill patients with injections of insulin.

Her first murder is believed to have occurred in 2007 when she killed a World War 2 veteran who was being looked after at Caressant Care. Elizabeth Wettlaufer killed eight patients in various places and attempted to kill a further six. In 2016, Wettlaufer checked into a drug rehabilitation centre and confessed to her crimes. She said the motivation for the murders was a strange 'surge' and compulsion which she couldn't control. Wettlaufer said that when this surge gripped her she could hear cackling laughter which seemed to be coming from the bowels of hell. Elizabeth Wettlaufer was clearly highly disturbed and just about the last person in the world you'd want working in a medical care home.

Staff who worked with Wettlaufer later said she was a friendly woman who would often bring the patients gifts. They had no idea that she was secretly killing them. Wettlaufer, like other Angel of Mercy medical killers, was said to be obsessed with death and intoxicated with the power she had over the fate of her patients. She had this deluded sense that she was sparing people from pain by killing them.

Wettlaufer was charged formally with eight counts of murder and (later) six more charges consisting of four counts of attempted murder and two counts of aggravated assault. Elizabeth Wettlaufer was then sentenced to life imprisonment and later sent to a secure facility in Montreal to receive medical treatment. In a report on the case, Commissioner Eileen E. Gillese admitted that Elizabeth Wettlaufer might not have been caught if she hadn't confessed (which was a rather disturbing admission). 'The evidence,' said Gillese, 'showed that no one suspected that Wettlaufer was intentionally harming those under her care — not the residents or their families, not those who worked alongside Wettlaufer, and not those who managed and supervised her.'

Elizabeth Wettlaufer was found to be suffering from antisocial personality disorder and is believed to have killed the patients purely for her own gratification. Ultimately, this was a highly disturbed and troubled woman who couldn't seem to distinguish right from wrong anymore. If she hadn't been caught there is no telling how many people she might have killed in the end. This case received much publicity in Canada because it was revealed that Wettlaufer's previous infractions at medical facilities were not reported to the College of Nurses of Ontario. If they had been she might have been banned from working as a nurse much sooner and thus prevented some of these tragedies.

BEVERLEY ALLITT was a nurse who killed four infants and children and tried to kill many more. She is a deeply disturbed and dangerous woman. Alliitt was born in Lincolnshire in 1968. She was pretty odd from a young age and would fake illness to get attention. She famously had a healthy healthy appendix removed for no reason - such was her ability to pretend she was poorly or suffering from something. Allitt trained to be a nurse as a young woman and despite her poor attendance record, an incident where she was suspected of smearing excrement on a wall, and failing her nursing exams, she managed to secure a position at Grantham and Kesteven Hospital in Lincolnshire in 1991.

Allitt's first victim was seven-week-old Liam Taylor. She was caring for Liam when he began suffering from breathing problems. He eventually ended up on life support with brain damage and his parents had to give their consent to turn the machine off. The alarm monitors had not sounded when Liam stopped breathing but although this was (in hindsight) suspicious at the time no foul play was suspected. Two weeks later 11-year- old Timothy Hardwick died in Allitt's care when his heart stopped. Timothy suffered from cerebral palsy and his death was felt to have been a consequence of his epilepsy.

The next victim was one-year-old Kayley Desmond. Kayley was making good progress after being admitted to the hospital with a chest infection but she went into cardiac arrest while Allitt was looking after her. The staff noticed a puncture mark near Kaley's armpit indicative of an injection but - once again - no foul play was suspected. Allitt continued to prey on children in the hospital. Five year-old Paul Crampton suffered from insulin shock while in the care of Allitt. He was sent to another hospital and thankfully managed to survive. Amazingly, Allitt was the nurse who looked after him during the journey. She still wasn't suspected of anything.

A day later five-year-old Bradley Gibson went into cardiac arrest at the hospital but was saved. On two occasions he was found to have dangerously high levels on insulin and his main nurse was (of course) Beverley Allitt. That same day two-year-old Yik Hung Chan nearly died in the hospital after his oxygen levels dropped alarmingly. On the 1st of April, two-month-old Becky Phillips died in the hospital from convulsions. Becky had only been admitted for a stomach virus. Her sister was admitted for tests but stopped breathing while at the hospital. By now the authorities should have deduced that foul play was involved in all these strange and tragic incidents.

About three weeks later 15 month old Claire Peck was treated at the hospital for asthma and suffered a cardiac arrest while on a ventilator. Clare was brought into a stable condition but tragically died of another cardiac arrest shortly after. The nurse looking after her was Beverley Allitt. Traces of Lignocaine were found in Clare's system after tests. This is a drug for heart problems but it is never prescribed for children. This naturally raised all manner of alarm bells in the hospital. The investigation deduced that a common denominator in the incidents was that the children had dangerously high levels of insulin. It was no coincidence that Allitt had reported the key to the insulin cabinet was missing.

There were also missing nursing logs - which was obviously suspicious. The other common demonitator in this case was Beverley Alitt. The hospital soon realised that she had been looking after all the children who died or nearly died. Allitt had attacked thirteen children over a 59 day period and killed four of them. She was sentenced to 13 concurrent terms of life imprisonment in 1993 and sent to Rampton Secure Hospital. Allitt was deemed to be suffering from Munchausen's Syndrome by Proxy. Munchausen syndrome by proxy (MSBP) is a mental health problem in which a caregiver makes up or causes an illness or injury in a person under his or her care.

COLIN NORRIS was born in Glasgow in 1976. Norris worked in a travel agency when he left school but he decided he wanted to do something different in the end so he trained to be a nurse. He studied for a Higher Nursing Diploma at Dundee University's School of Nursing and Midwifery and then worked at the Royal Victoria Hospital, Dundee on a placement scheme. Norris also spent some time working in a nursing home. The experiences of Colin Norris in the hospital and nursing home were not to his liking because he was working with geriatric patients.

Norris, it seems, didn't like caring for old people very much. He especially disliked having to bathe elderly female patients. Norris was gay and it has been speculated that it made him uncomfortable having to wash female patients but it seems unlikely that his sexuality had anything to do with it. It was more the case that Norris wanted to work in a more general (and 'exciting' - as he put it himself) medical environment rather than simply look after old people. While Norris is alleged to have had a distaste for elderly patients there is no evidence that he harmed any of them in his student nurse years.

Much is made in this case of the fact that while he was training to be a nurse, Norris was taught about the story of Jessie McTavish. Jessie McTavish was a Glasgow nurse who was convicted in 1974 of murdering a patient with insulin. McTavish had learned that insulin was soluble and thus a potential homicide agent in which one might plausibly get away with the crime (she was obviously wrong about the second part of this deduction). The case of Jessie McTavish is said to have stuck with Colin Norris and inspired his own alleged medical crimes. Added to this was the fact that as part of his training he was taught how to care for patients with diabetes.

After his training was completed in Dundee, Norris got a job as a staff nurse at Leeds General Infirmary in Yorkshire. Norris would also work at St James's University Hospital in the city too. It was here in Leeds that his crimes took place. Norris is alleged to have been frustrated and unhappy at having to care for some elderly patients on his ward in Leeds. It is said that he tried to kill 90 year old Vera Wilby by way of insulin overdose in 2002 but she actually survived this murder attempt. In June of that same year, Norris was later found in court to have killed Bridget Bourke, 88, and then in October he murdered Irene Crookes, 79. These women were judged to have been killed by insulin overdose - despite the fact that they were not diabetic.

At the time of the deaths no foul play was suspected by the hospital - although Colin Norris was starting to get noticed by the staff. One colleague would later say that Norris seemed quite amused when a patient died - which was certainly what you could describe as odd and unprofessional behaviour for a nurse. Norris was also said to be bad tempered with the elderly patients on his ward and not exactly a barrel of laughs in his treatment of these ailing old folk. At his later trial there were many accounts by colleagues and patients about Norris being angry and verbally abusive with elderly patients on the wards.

Norris was also later accused of murdering 86-year-old Ethel Hall on his ward. The trouble began for Colin Norris when Ethel Hall was found unconscious. Dr Emma Ward found that Hall, who was being treated for a broken hip, had been given 1,000 units of insulin. A diabetic is usually given 50 units (not that Mrs Hall was even a diabetic anyway). This was all highly suspicious and alarming and so an investigation was launched by the police.

The police found that 18 deaths at the hospital were - retrospectively - deemed to be suspicious and that a common denominator in these deaths is that they often seemed to occur during the shifts of Colin Norris. Another salient detail was that these incidents seemed to occur at weekends or very early in the morning. In other words they took place at a time when specialist staff would be less likely to be there. Was that a coincidence or did it indicate something more sinister?

The police case against Norris judged that he was the only person who worked those specific shifts (where the incidents took place) and who had access to those patients and insulin. He was also the only nurse who worked on the two wards where the deaths took place. Much was made too of the fact that Norris had once predicted when a patient would die and been proved completely accurate in this prediction. Norris would claim this was simply some dark humour which was blown out of all proportion. What didn't help Norris though was that he confessed to this 'prediction' in a police interview but then denied it in court. That was obviously a contradiction.

During the police investigation into Norris he was suspended from work on full pay. He even went abroad a few times during this period and enjoyed some holidays. Those who were close to Norris said he was scared though at the thought that he might end up in prison. The police conducted a number of interviews with Norris and one particular detail struck them as a big red flag. Norris claimed that the insulin which was taken from the fridge in the hospital without permission and then used on the patients must have been stolen by an intruder while the nurses were busy or taking a break.

Presumably then this alleged intruder, according to Colin Norris, must have injected the patients too. This all struck the police as pure fiction. It was rather implausible to think that someone would sneak into a hospital somehow unobserved and then - for reasons best known to themselves - attempt to kill elderly patients with overdoses of insulin. Added to this was the fact that the insulin fridge was locked with a key code which was only known to the medical staff. The police believed that Colin Norris was simply making this up. They didn't believe he was telling the truth in his interviews.

The police also found Colin Norris to be something of a cold fish in that he showed no sorrow whatsoever for the deaths of these old people on the wards. Norris told the police he couldn't even remember these patients. Norris was combative and arrogant in his dealings with the police. He treated them with disdain and said they had no case against him.

Norris became quite obstreperous at times during his trial at Newcastle. Those who believe he is innocent might argue that this was perfectly natural in the circumstances. If you were charged with crimes you didn't commit then anger and frustration would be understandable.

Norris was found guilty of four murders on an 11-1 majority verdict. One member of the jury was clearly not convinced that Norris was a killer. Norris got life with a minimum of 30 years. Usually with medical killers they are found to be highly disturbed individuals with dark pasts who become addicted to the power they wield as medical professions. They like to play God with the lives of their patients. A number of other medical killers in history did their crimes for financial reasons in that they wanted to get their grubby mitts on the money and valuables of their patients. Colin Norris didn't really fit these patterns though. He was a reasonably normal sort of person whose main motive seemed to be that these elderly patients got on his nerves.

Colin Norris was called 'evil' by the police and judge. He was (inevitably) compared to Harold Shipman in the media. In the years since the conviction of Colin Norris though there has been a concerted campaign to overturn his conviction. Some scientific experts believe his conviction was unsafe and that the evidence against him was circumstantial. Those that convicted Norris though remain convinced that he was a ruthless medical killer. In 2021 his case was referred to the court of appeals. It remains to be seen if Norris will ever prove his innocence or whether he was guilty all along. Colin Norris and his family still believe that one day he will be free again and his convictions will be quashed.

KIMBERLY CLARK SAENZ was born in Fall River, Massachusetts in 1973. Saenz was another of those awful medical killers. She used her position as a nurse to murder patients. Saenz killed five patients and is believed to have attempted to murder five more. Although she was married with two children, Saenz was a troubled woman who was hooked on prescription drugs and had a conviction for public intoxication. Saenz had a battery of nursing jobs in her life but was fired more than once. She was dismissed from one hospital for stealing Demerol and then trying to fake the drug test she was subsequently obliged to take.

Saenz ended up at DaVita's Lufkin clinic in Texas - which dealt with patients on dialysis. A strangely high number of patients at the clinic began to suffer from cardiac problems after Saenz began working there. Paramedics were bewildered and very concerned by this sudden spike in cardiac incidents and asked the hospital to launch an investigation. DaVita consequently sent some surveyors to the clinic to see if they could find out what the problem was. The investigation established that Kimberly Clark Saenz had been on shift for 85% of the cardiac emergencies. This was clearly highly suspicious and probably not a coincidence.

Two patients then gave statements in which they claimed they had seen Saenz injecting other patients with sodium hypochlorite. Sodium hypochlorite is better known as bleach. The clinic was closed after syringes used by Saenz showed clear traces of bleach. It was then established that in google searches on the personal computer of Saenz she had researched if bleach could kill someone if it was injected. Other nurses also gave accounts of how Saenz would talk about which patients she didn't like and show no remorse when they went into cardiac arrest or died.

Although this all sounds like an open and shut case it wasn't quite that simple in the end. There was relatively little scientific research in detecting bleach in the blood so they had to get in scientific experts to build a case. These experts had to prove and explain how an agent like bleach would produce a reaction in the body that could result in cardiac arrest. They thankfully managed to do this in the end. Prosecutors wanted the death penalty for Saenz but at her 2012 trial she received life in prison. Kimberly Clark Saenz appealed her conviction in 2015 but to no avail. The evidence against her at the trial was simply too overwhelming and conclusive.

TIMEA FALUDI was born in Hungary in 1977. She was a nurse at the Gyula Nviro Hospital in Budapest and was convicted of murdering dozens of patients. Faludi joined the staff in 1994 and the deaths occurred during the night shifts she worked. She worked at the hospital for six years without raising any alarms and mostly cared for patients who were terminally ill. Faludi became an experienced nurse who was well liked by her colleagues and seemed very professional and good at her job. This all changed though when a colleague saw Faludi giving patients intravenous injections without a doctor's prescription.

Euthanasia is illegal in Hungary and she was arrested. Faludi confessed to killing forty patients when she was arrested but then seemed to retract this confession. The authorities could only find evidence for around ten deaths (a lot of the victims had obviously been cremated) - although it seems to be a fairly agreed fact that she killed a lot more people than that.

Faludi claimed that she killed because she wanted to relieve the suffering of patients but prosecutors begged to differ and believed that, like other medical killers, Faludi had developed a God complex and become intoxicated with the power she had over the life and death of patients. Faludi's crimes were mitigated by the fact that the patients she killed were apparently terminally ill. It is for this reason that she received a fairly light sentence of nine years (and was of course banned from ever becoming a nurse again). Was she a cold blooded killer or pure Angel of Mercy?

The case against Faludi would point out that her evidence was full of contradictions because she kept changing it (it seems plausible that her lawyers were the main culprits in this). There is also the fact that the patients she killed, while they might have been ill, did not give their consent for their lives to be terminated (in many cases they were incapable of this). Would Faludi have killed if she had been caring for non terminal patients? We may already know the answer to that question because two of her victims were not terminally ill and simply waiting for surgery.

The court verdict on Faludi stated that - "She alternately put herself in the place of the doctor or in that of the patient and took decisions instead of them. The term euthanasia can only be used at all if a patient expresses a wish to have his or her life terminated. In Faludi's cases, this did not happen." The court called Faludi a rational intelligent women who was trustworthy on the surface but secretly believed she was God. Faludi, who was 25 at the time of the trial, tends to be known as The Black Angel in Hungary. She was released from prison in 2009 and (understandably) maintains a low profile these days.

LUDIVINE CHAMBERT was born in France in 1983. Chambet worked in a number of nursing homes around Jacob-Bellecombette in Savoie and was the employed at Chambéry hospital. Chambet had a form of gigantism which gave her a very oversized body and some deformations. As a result of this she suffered from ridicule at school - which must have left mental scars. She was later an unlicensed nursing assistant and seemed like a perfectly kind and caring woman to those that knew her.

It is speculated that Chamet's mental health began to erode after the death of her mother in 2013. Chambet was exceptionally close to her mother and felt lost and adrift in the world after her mother passed away. Chambet had no friends or love life and her world revolved around her mother. After her mother passed away, she suffered from a deep depression and - eventually - began to do some unexplainable and tragic things.

Chambet began killing patients in the nursing home l'Ehpad du Césalet at Chambéry she worked in by giving them large quantities of drugs like neuroleptics and antidepressants. These patients, many of whom were elderly, feel into comas from which they never recovered. The patients killed by Chambet were not terminal and would have got better were it not for Chambet murdering them. What rumbled Chambet was the death of an 83 year-old woman who had Parkinsons. The nursing home had experienced a number of patient deaths which seemed somewhat mysterious and they soon deduced that the common factor was Ludivine Chambet.

Chambet had been on duty for all of these slightly strange patient deaths.

In 2013, Chambet was arrested. She confessed to killing a number of patients but said she had done so to alleviate their suffering. This defence is one that all medical serial killers seem to use and in Chambet's case, as with most others, it simply didn't wash. What had really killed these patients it seems was Chambet's descent into mental illness. In 2017 Ludivine Chambet was found guilty of ten homicides and sentenced to 25 years in prison.

Chambet's treatment by the authorities was humane because of her obvious fragility and mental health problems. It was argued in court that she wasn't really a serial killer because, in her deluded mind, she thought she was helping these patients. However, Chambet did say that she was compelled to kill by a split version of herself she called the 'personality'. A number of serial killers have said something like this after they were captured. Though convicted of ten murders, investigators at the trial believe that Ludivine Chambet probably killed thirteen people. She clearly would have killed a lot more if she hadn't been caught. Ludivine Chambet became known as The Poisoner of Chambéry in the French media.

RETA MAYS is an American former nursing assistant who was convicted of murdering seven elderly veterans in her care at the Louis A. Johnson VA Medical Center in Clarksburg, West Virginia. Mays was born on September 28, 1975, in West Virginia. She worked as a nursing assistant at the VA Medical Center between 2015 and 2018. During this time, she administered insulin to patients who were not diabetic, leading to severe hypoglycemia and death.

The murders came to light in 2018 when a series of unexplained deaths at the facility raised suspicion. An investigation was launched, and it was discovered that Mays had intentionally caused the deaths of the veterans by administering insulin injections without medical need. In 2020, Mays pleaded guilty to seven counts of second-degree murder and one count of assault with intent to commit murder. She expressed remorse for her actions and admitted to betraying the trust placed in her as a healthcare professional.

March 2021, Mays was sentenced to life in prison without the possibility of parole. The case shocked the nation and raised concerns about the safety of veterans in healthcare facilities.

THE BEST (OR SHOULD THAT BE WORST?) OF THE REST

Despite the grisly gallery of poisoners we've discussed so far, we have in fact barely scratched the surface. You'd need several books to cover all the poisoning cases in true crime history. We'll do our best in this chapter to highlight some of the most salient cases we've yet to discuss. FLORENCE MAYBRICK was an American woman who gained notoriety in the late 19th century due to her involvement in a murder case. She was accused of poisoning her husband, James Maybrick, with arsenic in 1889 in Liverpool. During the trial, it was revealed that Florence Maybrick had purchased arsenic, which was commonly used as a medicine at the time, and had administered it to her husband. However, the case was complex, and there were conflicting testimonies and evidence presented. Florence Maybrick claimed that her husband had been a habitual user of arsenic and that she had only given him small doses as a tonic.

Despite her defense, Florence Maybrick was found guilty of murder and initially sentenced to death. However, her sentence was later commuted to life imprisonment. After serving 15 years in prison, she was released and returned to the United States. The Florence Maybrick case remains a subject of debate and controversy, with differing opinions on her guilt or innocence. Some argue that she was wrongly convicted, while others believe she was indeed responsible for her husband's death. The case highlights the complexities of historical criminal trials and the challenges in determining the truth in such matters.

This story gets weirder still though. In 1992, a man named Michael Barrett claimed to have discovered the diary of Jack the Ripper in Liverpool. The diary revealed that the Ripper was Liverpool cotton merchant James Maybrick - the person believed to have been poisoned by Florence. Maybrick was not a Ripper suspect at the time of the murders but the (retrospective) theory is that he was driven into a woman hating rage by his wife and thus became Jack the Ripper.

The question of whether or not Maybrick could have been Jack the Ripper obviously comes down to the authenticity of the diary. How very convenient of the Ripper to leave a diary! You can forgive people for being a trifle on the dubious side about this alleged Ripper memoir. Those Hitler diaries seemed too good to be true too and we all know what happened there. Michael Barrett initially said he purchased the diary in a pub but then his wife contradicted this and said it had been in the family for yonks.

It seems to be the consensus (though others would disagree) that the Ripper diary is questionable at best and might well be fake. Michael Barrett later said it was forged but his wife then disputed this and Barrett did an about turn and said it wasn't faked. Forensic tests on the diary tend to suggest the paper was very old but the ink could have come from any time. Some believe the diary might be real and others think it's a fake designed to make money. It is difficult not to suspect the latter theory.

There are certainly some inaccuracies in the diaries in relation to the Ripper murders and the text feels somewhat bogus and hokey. Here's a sample - 'I am fighting a battle within me. My desire for revenge is overwhelming. The whore has destroyed my life. I try whenever possible to keep all sense of respectability. I worry so over Bobo and Gladys, no others matter. Tonight I will take more than ever. I miss the thrill of cutting them up. I do believe I have lost my mind. All the bitches will pay for the pain. Before I am finished all of England will know the name I have given myself. It is indeed a name to remember. It shall be, before long, on every persons lips within the land. Perhaps her gracious Majesty will become acquainted with it. I wonder if she will honour me with a knighthood ha ha.'

Does that really sound like a diary entry written by a well to do Victorian businessman? Well, not really, A year after the alleged diary was found, a watch alleging to have belonged to Maybrick was revealed and appeared to contain the initials of the Ripper victims. This watch was deemed to be more period authentic than the diaries. It remains the case though that many regard the evidence regarding Maybrick and the Ripper to be highly questionable. There is not much evidence in Maybrick's biographies that he was a secret murderer. The general theory for those inclined to believe that he was the Ripper is that his unfaithful wife Florence drove him insane and thus he became Jack the Ripper.

Interestingly, a BBC show called Murder, Mystery and My Family examined the death of James Maybrick and came to the conclusion that his wife Florence Maybrick might have had an unfair trial (Magistrates at the time tended to be biased in favour of men). It is possible that medication James Maybrick was on might have been a big contributor to his death - which opens the door to the possibility that his wife wasn't a cold blooded poisoner. James Maybrick died in 1889 so if you do believe he could have been the Ripper this is one thing in your favour because it would explain why the Ripper murders ceased.

Believe it or not, the Ripper is not the only elusive serial killer alleged to have been James Maybrick. Between 1884 and 1885, a killer known as The Servant Girl Annihilator killed at least eight people in Austin, Texas. William Sydney Porter, better known as the short story writer O. Henry, was the person who coined the nickname of this killer. The Servant Girl Annihilator deployed an axe to kill six women, an eleven-year-old girl and one man. Several other people were injured in attacks. Six of the victims were black and the unfortunate victims of the killer were usually attacked in their beds (when they were obviously at their most vulnerable). The victims were often dragged outside and mutilated.

The crime scenes were exceptionally gruesome with seemingly gallons of blood surrounding later victims. One victim had her head cleaved in half. As you might imagine these murders created a panic in Austin and around 400 men were arrested and questioned over the murders. Vigilante posses began to patrol at night searching for the fiend and huge rewards for the capture of the killer were offered. While the killer was never captured all of this combined activity did seemingly make The Servant Girl Annihilator cease his activities though and the murders came to a halt.

Although there were many eyewitness accounts of the killer (he was deemed to be white and quite short) no one was ever proven to have committed the murders. There is a theory (never proven of course) that The Servant Girl Annihilator was also Jack the Ripper and that three years after the Austin murders he moved to London and started killing again. There was a a similar sort of gruesome MO when it came to the murders in both cases but the Ripper never used an axe.

A cook from Malaysia named Maurice is often a suspect in this case because he worked in a hotel near where all but two of The Servant Girl Annihilator murders took place and then moved to London. As he was both in Austin and London at the time of the Annihilator and Ripper murders, this cook is often held up as evidence that both killers could have been one and the same. James Maybrick was also in Austin at the time of The Servant Girl Annihilator murders so he too is often used in theories which seek to prove that the Annihilator was also the Ripper.

All of this though is unproven and open to doubt. Modern perspectives on this case have suggested the Annihilator could have been Nathan Elgin. Elgin was a cook who worked near where the Austin murders took place. He was missing a toe - a distinction which matched a footprint found near one of the murders. Elgin was killed by the police in 1886 when he was caught trying to assault a girl with a knife. All of this suggests that Elgin is a strong retrospective suspect but whether or not he was really The Servant Girl Annihilator is impossible to say with complete certainty. As for James Maybrick, it seems highly unlikely that he was both of these killers and whether or not you think he was the Ripper comes down to how authentic you think the incriminating diary and watch alleged to belong to him are.

MADAME DE BRINVILLIERS was born in Paris in 1630. She was a French aristocrat who murdered her father and brothers in order to inherit their estates. However, it is often claimed that killed dozens of people in hospitals while testing and refining the poison which she would used to kill her relatives. The truth of this later claim is disputed but it wouldn't surprise you if it was true. Marquise de Brinvilliers was clearly a ruthless and ambitious woman who would stop at nothing to get what she wanted. You can't imagine she was the sort of person who would lose much sleep over some people in hospital getting poisoned.

The Marquise was the eldest of the children in her family but she was not in line to inherit the estate. As a woman she was expected to marry into wealth and not burden the family. She had marriages and children but the Marquise was very promiscuous and had many lovers. This is said to have rankled her father because he felt she was risking shame on the family reputation. The Marquise's father was very angry when he learned that his daughter was having an affair with a man named Godin de Sainte-Croix so he arranged for Sainte-Croix to be arrested. It is naturally speculated that this action made the Marquise angry enough to contemplate murdering her father.

Godin de Sainte-Croix started an alchemy business when he was released from prison. He remained in (clandestine you would imagine) contact with the Marquise and through Sainte-Croix she learned a great deal about chemicals and poisons. It is claimed that the Marquise now conducted a number of experiments with poison on a local hospital in Paris and also on her own servants. Up to thirty people are alleged to have died as a result of these experiments. The source for this claim is a police report although, as we have noted, not everyone believes this happened. One can certainly build a case for it though.

Noble French figures were often expected to visit hospitals and the Marquise would have had ample opportunity to poison patients. Suspicious deaths in hospitals at the time would hardly have been noticed or logged in the 1660s in the way they would today. People simply died a lot more often in those days than they do today. Medical treatment was primitive and disease was more rampant. The Marquise could have offed a number of patients and servants for all we know.

In 1666 she began to poison her father. The Marquise actually put an employee of hers in the family home to finish her father off with poison. Her father, shortly before his death, invited her home and so she actually finished him off herself in the end. The Marquise then set about poisoning her brothers. This was a lot more difficult because she wasn't on good terms with them and they barely spoke to her. They did though live in the family home so she got a footman employed by the family to help her. One of the brothers was poisoned with an apple pie and they managed to get to the other brother too in the end.

Strangely, the Marquise seemed to get away with the murders at first despite the fact that they were highly suspicious. She was rumbled though when Godin de Sainte-Croix died. He was found to have letters in his possession from the Marquise in which she'd promised him a sum of money after the deaths of her father and brothers had been completed. Case closed. The participation of La Chaussée, the footman who helped in the murders, was also deduced and he fled. When he was captured, La Chaussée admitted that the Marquise had been behind the deaths of her relatives. The Marquise went on the run and tried to hide in England. She was eventually arrested in Belgium.

The Marquise at first denied all knowledge of the murders and said she had nothing to do with them. She said that Godin de Sainte-Croix must have killed them. However, she was not believed and sentenced to death. The Marquise was subject to a torture known as water cure before her death. In this rather unpleasant practice the victim is forced to drink large quantities of water in a short time until their stomach is full and they can barely breathe. The Marquise was then beheaded with a sword in 1676. She was 45 years-old.

Discerning who the first serial killer in Britain was is no easy task but one of the earliest is alleged to have been a man named JONATHAN BALLS. Balls lived in the village of Happisburgh in Norfolk and the local legend goes that, as he entered old age, he started bumping off his grandchildren so that his children would be less distracted and have more time to look after him! Balls died in 1846 at the age of 82. He was an unpopular character and no one was too sad to see him shuttle off this mortal coil. His life had apparently been one of dishonesty and crime.

A suspiciously high number of relatives had already perished in this family. A granddaughter named Ann died in 1830 while daughter Maria died in 1935. Another granddaughter died in 1836 as an infant and in 1841 yet another granddaughter (thirteen month old Martha) also passed away. Adding to the misery was the death of Martha's three year-old brother William. Another grandson named Samuel also died as did Jonathan's wife Elizabeth. While the death of Elizabeth could be put down to old age there was no such explanation for why the young members of the family were dropping like flies.

Until that is it was discovered that Jonathan Balls had purchased large quantities of arsenic. This was for a supposed rat problem but true crime historians will be well aware that arsenic was the poison of choice for a large number of murderers in this and subsequent eras. There was naturally much local gossip about this apparently cursed family and how they kept dropping dead at a rate that was almost impossible to keep up with. Eventually it was decided that the multiple deaths were simply too suspicious and so the local coroner was badgered into ordering some exhumations.

Though an open verdict was recorded on some of the exhumations it was established that arsenic had been ingested by many of the young deceased in the Balls family. It was also pretty much established that Balls might have killed his sons too - who perished some years before. The odd thing about this case is that Jonathan Balls had apparently died of arsenic poisoning too. The story goes that he got fed up with local whispers and innuendo and so decided to end it all. He was an old man at the end of his life anyway and had no desire to end up in court on trial.

Jonathan Balls, in the later part of his life, was very dependent on his daughters to look after him and this is generally felt to have been the motive for these heartless murders. He wanted his daughters to focus all of their time on him rather than their children - though of course that didn't stop him from apparently bumping off a daughter too.

The London New Weekly Bell Messenger said of the case - 'The supposition is that he poisoned his grandchildren in order that their parents might be better able to support him. In addition to the many deaths charged against old Balls, it is now believed that he disposed of his two sons, who have been dead more than ten years, and his father and mother.' Heaven knows how many people 'old Balls' might have killed. He was like a character in an E.C Horror comics yarn.

GIULIA TOFANA was born in 1620 in Palermo. Tofana was the daughter of Thofania d'Amado - a woman who was executed for murdering her own husband. It is said that a few secrets on how to bump off men were passed down from mother to daughter. Giulia Tofana was a legendary poisoner who is alleged to have clocked up 600 victims (though this is unverifiable as records from the time are naturally difficult to get hold of and barely exist).

Giulia Tofana was what you might call a forerunner of Katharina Popova in that she offered a service whereby she would help unhappy wives kill their husbands. Giulia had a cosmetics product called Aqua Tofana which was essentially supposed to be an ointment for bad skin. This product however containe arsenic and other dangerous elements which meant it could be used as a poison. It was a clever way to disguise the method of murder for these wives.

'Another element of Giulia's poison that made it so masterfully deceitful is how it killed its victims,' wrote Syfy. 'The first dose, normally diluted with some kind of liquid, would cause exhaustion and physical weakness. The second dose would bring on stomach aches, vomiting, and dysentery. The third or fourth dose would take care of the rest. The poison, and the method of administering it, meant that doctors and investigators believed the death had been caused by some unknown illness or disease. The slow-nature of the poisoning meant that victims had a chance to get their affairs in order, and their wives were there to exert their influence over what that order looked like. And the deaths — those tragically young lives lost to their sickbeds — were never believed to be anything more. The poison undetectable, the murders free of suspicion, Giulia's business flourished.'

Giulia Tofana's daughter Girolama Spera was also a willing accomplice in this deadly scheme. The story goes that Giulia Tofana was caught when a wife put this deadly beauty product in her husband's soup but then had second thoughts and told him not to eat it. When he learned what was going on, the woman's husband made her go to the authorities and rat on Giulia Tofana. Tofana was given refuge in a local church at first but when a (false) rumour spread that she had poisoned the water supply in Rome she was arrested and tortured. Giulia Tofana confessed to six hundred murders but this figure is impossible to substantiate. We do know though that her activities were responsible for an awful lot of deaths. It is believed that Giulia Tofana and her daughter were executed. Their bodies were thrown from the church that had given them shelter. It is sometimes reported that the composer Mozart was killed by means of Aqua Tofana but this is believed to be an urban myth.

THE CROYDON POISONER case relates to a case in 1928 and 1929 where three members of a fairly well to do Croydon family in England were apparently poisoned. However, the mystery of who was behind the murders was never actually solved. The first to die was 59 year-old Edmund Duff. Duff used to be the High Commissioner for Nigeria. He had eaten a dinner of chicken and potatoes (many accounts of this case believe the poison was put in the beer he drank with his meal) and soon after began complaining that he felt sick and was suffering from cramps.

The stomach ailment of Edmund Duff rapidly got worse and he suffered from diarrhea and escalating pain. A doctor was called out but Edmund expired that same night. Dr Binning, who tried to treat him, was rather suspicious of the circumstances of this sudden ill health and didn't rule out poisoning. Ten months later Edmund's sister in law Vera Sydney also died in similar circumstances. She fell ill after eating her lunch of soup and died in near identical fashion to Edmund. Vera's death was put down to a gastric complaint. Her mother and the family cat had partaken in some of the soup and fell ill too but they both recovered.

A month later Vera's mother Violet Sydney wasn't so lucky and also died. You can probably guess what happened. That's right. She had just eaten when she was overwhelmed by dreadful stomach pains and a feeling of sickness. An examination after her death found no obvious reason for why she had died. The surviving relatives were by now understandably suspicious of these sudden deaths and demanded that a more thorough investigation should take place. They kicked up sufficient fuss for exhumations to take place and - sure enough - that familiar true crime villain arsenic was found to be the culprit. But who was the poisoner? That was the most pressing question facing the authorities.

The Croydon case literally became like a game of Cluedo at this point. Everyone was a suspect at first. All the maids and servants had to be ruled out and all the surviving relatives had to be investigated. The police found some weed killer in the house but deducing who purchased this weed killer or whether it could have been used as a poison was no easy task. It was generally established that the first victim was killed through beer, the second through soup, and the last via some medicine she was taking. This meant that the killer had to have access to all three people and also have a motive to kill them. Well, believe it or not, no one was ever charged with the murders. The police simply didn't find sufficient evidence to build a case against anyone. There was a main suspect though. This was Edmund's wife Grace.

The general theory is that Grace had fallen in love with another man and wanted to get rid of her husband. That did pose the question though of why Grace killed the other relatives - an act which would surely attract more suspicion. The police visited the home of Grace's brother and found that he had rat poison and weed killer in the house. Did he conspire with Grace in these murders? The police obviously didn't think so because they ruled him out of their enquires. The same could not be said of Grace. The police always suspected that she did it but they simply couldn't prove it beyond doubt. At the inquest into the deaths Grace was questioned and said nothing that incriminated her. Grace died in 1973 at a ripe old age. She was always suspected of being The Croydon Poisoner but no charges were ever brought against her.

When it comes to MADAME POPOVA, not much is known about the background or true age of Katharina Popova but we do know she came from Samara - a city in southwestern Russia, framed by the Volga and Samara rivers. Motivated by her own unhappy marriage, Popova set up a service whereby she would rid unhappy women of unwanted husbands by murdering them! Believe it or not, this business (which was obviously operated on a secret need to know basis) flourished for thirty years and claimed hundreds of victims.

Popova is said to have participated in many of the murders herself by engineering an acquaintance with the husband and then slipping him some arsenic. On other occasions a hitman was sometimes dispatched to do away with the husband in question. If you wanted to get rid of a husband and employed Popova you had to pay her half the fee up front and then the other half once the murder was completed. A surprisingly high number of women took advantage of this unusual and lethal business to get rid of husbands.

The highly successful if unorthodox business run by Katharina Popova came an end when a woman who paid for her husband to be murdered felt such dreadful remorse and guilt over the death that she went to the authorities and told them all about Popova and what had happened. When word got out about Popova's activities an angry mob descended and would have been perfectly happy to lynch her. Popova was calm though despite her capture. She said she was proud of what she had done and felt great pride in liberating hundreds of women from unhappy marriages.

Popova also proudly declared that she had never killed a single woman and that all the victims were men (as if that somehow excused her crimes! - they were ONLY men). Popova also seemed to be under the deluded belief that her murders had been very humane because she used or supplied poison. I'm fairly sure the person being poisoned didn't find it very humane! Popova had to be escorted to prison by armed soldiers to keep the unruly mob at bay. She was executed by firing squad in March 1909.

DR HAWLEY CRIPPEN was born in Coldwater, Michigan, in 1862, and pursued a career in medicine. He emigrated to England in 1897, where he soon established himself as a respected homeopathic practitioner. Crippen's life appeared to be that of an average middle-class Victorian - a loving husband and a mild-mannered doctor. However, behind this facade lay a dark secret that would unravel in the most sensational manner. Crippen's downfall began when he met Ethel Le Neve, a young typist at his medical practice. The two soon developed an intimate relationship, and it wasn't long before rumours began to circulate that Crippen's wife, Cora, had disappeared under mysterious circumstances. As the rumours grew louder, the authorities were drawn into the case, and a thorough investigation was launched.

What followed was an international manhunt that gripped the

imagination of people around the world. Crippen and Le Neve had fled to Belgium, using fake passports, but their escape was short-lived. The captain of the transatlantic passenger liner SS Montrose, on which they were travelling, became suspicious of their behaviour and alerted the authorities. The couple was arrested upon their arrival in Canada, and news of their capture spread like wildfire. The subsequent trial of Dr Crippen became a media frenzy, with reporters from around the globe flocking to London to cover the proceedings.

It was an unprecedented spectacle, as the public followed every twist and turn of the trial with bated breath. The evidence against Crippen was damning - a piece of human flesh found in the cellar of his home, identified as belonging to his wife, and traces of a poisonous substance in her remains. The doctor was found guilty of murder and sentenced to death by hanging. The Crippen case was a watershed moment in criminal history. It represented a turning point in the public's fascination with true crime, as newspapers and tabloids exploited the sensational details of the case for their own gain. It also marked the beginning of a new era in forensic science, with the use of forensic toxicology and the identification of human remains becoming crucial in solving crimes.

However, as time went on, doubts began to emerge regarding the evidence against Crippen. Some experts questioned the accuracy of the forensic analysis, while others argued that the human remains found at his home might not have been his wife's. These doubts led to a posthumous re-evaluation of the case, and in 2007, a team of forensic scientists revisited the evidence. They concluded that the remains found at Crippen's home did not belong to Cora Crippen, casting doubt on his guilt. The case of Dr Hawley Crippen remains a fascinating enigma, a story that continues to intrigue us over a century later.

HELENE JEGADO was born near Lorient in Brittany in 1803. She came from a family of servants and after the death of her mother was sent to assist two aunts in various places. Jégado worked as a servant or cook in various houses and even religious retreats. She did though have one compulsive weakness which she couldn't seem to resist at times.

Hélène Jégado was a poisoner who is believed to possibly killed as many as 36 people in all. Jégado poisoned for the first time in 1833 when she was employed by a priest.
Several members of the household were poisoned - including the aforementioned priest. Even the visiting sister of Hélène Jégado was poisoned.

Hélène Jégado did not attract any suspicion at this time because her grief at the deaths and poisonings was so convincing. She was clearly a highly accomplished actress. Jégado stayed at various places in the months and weeks that followed and death and illness was (suspiciously) never too far away. She poisoned her aunt, her landlady and the landlady's daughter, and later a widow she rented a room from. In 1935 she was employed at a new house and our deaths soon abounded.

It is said that Hélène Jégado even joined a convent. As you might imagine, as soon she started at the convent the nuns started dropping like flies. Oddly, Hélène Jégado apparently did not poison anyone from 1841 to 1849. It is unusual for serial killers to have long 'rest periods' like this but not unheard of. In 1850, Hélène Jégado began working for Théophile Bidard, who was a professor at the University of Rennes. When the servants started to fall ill and in some cases perished, suspicion finally began to fall on Hélène Jégado because she was usually the one caring for them at the time of their death.

Like many notorious poisoners, Hélène Jégado would offer to care for victims so she could maintain control over them and finish them off. When the local authorities decided to speak to Hélène Jégado they found it suspicious that she immediately announced her innocence before they'd even accused her of anything or explained why they had come to speak to her. Hélène Jégado was a difficult person to convict because they found no arsenic in her possessions and she had no clothing, valuables, or jewellery from her victims. She was either good at hiding her tracks or simply wasn't a financial serial killer.

It is often suggested that Hélène Jégado killed people who irritated her. This is certainly not uncommon in these strange and baffling cases of serial poisoners. They often seem to poison and kill people for fairly petty things like slights or little arguments. Hélène Jégado, though suspected of dozens of murders, was put on trial on three counts of murder and found guilty. Jégado gave an eccentric performance in court. She ranted and raved and insisted that she'd never poisoned anyone in her life. Her protestations of innocence did not stand up to too much scrutiny in court. She was executed by guillotine in front of a large crowd of onlookers on the Champ-de-Mars in Rennes in 1852.

CHRISTIANA EDMUNDS was born on November 26, 1829, in Margate, Kent. Edmunds gained notoriety for her role in poisoning people with strychnine-laced chocolates. She led a seemingly ordinary life as a spinster living with her father, but she developed an obsession with a married man named Charles Beard, whom she believed reciprocated her love. In 1871, Edmunds began purchasing chocolates from various shops and adulterating them with strychnine. She then distributed these tainted treats to people she believed were interfering in her relationship with Beard, including his wife and several neighbours. Tragically, three individuals who consumed the poisoned chocolates died as a result.

Suspicion initially fell on local confectioners for the poisonous chocolates, but eventually, the authorities discovered evidence pointing towards Edmunds. She was subsequently arrested and brought to trial in March 1872. During her trial, Edmunds attempted to plead insanity, claiming delusion and jealousy as the reasons for her crimes. Nevertheless, she was found guilty of murder and sentenced to death. However, her sentence was commuted to life imprisonment due to doubts about her mental state.

Following her conviction, Edmunds spent the remainder of her life institutionalized. She was initially placed in Broadmoor Hospital and later transferred to the West Riding Lunatic Asylum. She died there on September 1, 1907, at the age of 77. The case of Christiana Edmunds stands as a chilling example of how obsession and jealousy can drive an individual to commit heinous acts. Her use of chocolates, a seemingly innocent and pleasurable treat, to carry out her crimes shocked Victorian society and left a lasting mark on criminal history.

MARTHA RENDELL was born in 1871 in Australia. This was an awful woman by any standards who responsible for terrible crimes that begger belief. Rendell was the common-law wife of a man named Thomas Morris and murdered his three young children. The method in which she did this was exceptionally cruel. Rendell swabbed their throats with spirits of salts (hydrochloric acid). This caused inflammation and haemorrhage of the bowel. The throats of the children became inflamed to the point where they could no longer eat. They all died agonising and slow deaths.

Seven year-old Annie was the first victim and then Rendell did the same to Olive (aged five) and Arthur (aged fourteen). The family doctor though could find no evidence of anything suspicious about the deaths at first. This was clearly incompetence on his part. Martha Rendell's wicked and unfathomable crimes only came to light when she tried to do the same to the remaining son George. George got suspicious though and ran away. The police got involved in a search for George and when they found him the boy told them that Rendell had killed his siblings and was now trying to poison him with spirits of salts.

Exhumations of George's siblings took place and foul play was (not before time you might suggest) finally discovered. Diluted hydrochloric acid was found to be present in the throat tissue of the dead children. Martha Rendell pretended to be innocent and claimed a doctor had prescribed spirits of salts for the children but her defence was flimsy to say the least. Thomas Morris was actually charged with the murders too but he was acquitted in the end. These dreadful crimes had been the work of Martha Rendell alone.

As you can imagine, there was a lot of public anger in Australia when these hideous crimes came to light. The public would happily have lynched Martha Rendell given half a chance. There was never much danger of her getting anything but the sternest sentence possible. Rendell was hanged in Fremantle Prison on October the 6th, 1909. She was the last woman to be hanged in Western Australia. Her motivation for murder is presumed to have been the fact that she didn't like the children very much and resented having to share her husband's time and attention with them. So she simply decided to kill them in an exceptionally cruel way.

Before her execution, she declared 'I most solemnly wish to state that on this, the last morning of my life. I am innocent before God and man of having done anything that injured the children in any degree. The spirits of salts were never used by me on the children. If I had done it, I would confess. I believe it would be contrary to my most solemn convictions to profess to man to be innocent when before God I should be found guilty, which would be to me dying with a lie on my lips and a crime on my soul unconfessed — unforgiven. I pray to God to give me grace to forgive those who have sworn falsely my life away.' As that statement suggests, Martha Rendell never showed any remorse for her crimes. Despite the overwhelming evidence she went to the gallows still pretending to be innocent.

JOHANN OTTO HOCH was born on March 15, 1863, in Germany. Hoch immigrated to the United States in the late 1880s and settled in Chicago, Illinois. He would later earn the nickname "Marriage Killer" or "Bluebeard" due to his pattern of marrying multiple women and then murdering them for financial gain. Hoch would use various aliases and charm to court and marry vulnerable women, often widows or those with assets. His true intentions were to gain control of their finances and then dispose of them through poisoning or other means. He would typically poison his victims by lacing their food or drinks with arsenic. Hoch was skilled at avoiding suspicion by switching locations, names, and eluding law enforcement.

However, his reign of terror would eventually come to an end. In 1905, Hoch was arrested in New York City after an investigation raised suspicion about him. He was subsequently charged with the murder of one of his wives, Marie Walcker, and later convicted. During his trial, it was revealed that Hoch had married at least 55 women throughout his life and was thought to be responsible for the deaths of several more. He was sentenced to life in prison but died in 1906 from causes reported to be tuberculosis.

JAROSLAVA FABIANOVA is a Czech serial killer born in 1965 in Děčín. Like most serial killers she had an unpleasant childhood and suffered sexual abuse. In the early 1980s she joined a gang who took part in theft and prostitution. Fabiánová began her life of crime as a thief and took part in burglaries. She was gay in real life but had male clients in her duties as a prostitute. It was for the murder of some of these clients that she became an infamous figure in Czech true crime circles.

One can see why Jaroslava Fabiánová is sometimes dubbed the Czech Aileen Wuornos. Fabiánová, who was blonde and rather haggard looking, even resembled Wuornos somewhat in her appearance. Her first victim was a 78 year-old man who had visited Fabiánová for sexual services but then tried to avoid giving her any money. Fabiánová struck him three times with a hammer and then stabbed him over twenty times. It was a very frenzied and violent attack. Fabiánová was arrested for the murder but because of her age (she was not yet a legal adult) she only served four years in prison.

Upon her release, Fabiánová went back to prostitution and would often rob her clients. These included a number of foreign tourists. This sort of sideline was not quite as risky as it might sound because if you were a foreign tourist who has been robbed by a prostitute you probably wouldn't necessarily want to report it to the police for all manner of reasons- legality and embarrassment being the most obvious.

Fabiánová landed in prison again after drugging a client so she could steal his money. The man died of cardiac arrest as a result of the drugs she'd put in his drink. She was sentenced to ten years in prison but, once again, got off quite lightly and only served about five years in the end. Unbelievably, she is said to have then served another short prison sentence for stealing a telephone. Jaroslava Fabiánová was the ultimate jailbird.

In 2003, Jaroslava Fabiánová went back to her old murderous ways when she killed an elderly man named Augustin Kůra in his apartment. He had been struck with a meat cleaver and Fabiánová had then stolen some paintings and valuable tools from his home. Fabiánová was stupid enough to try and sell the paintings herself and this began the process of putting the police onto her. Fabiánová then met a man named Richard Sýkora on a tram. He invited Fabiánová to his home and she stabbed him nearly forty times. She was pretty out of control by this time and highly dangerous.

By now a search warrant had been put out for Fabiánová and when the body of Richard Sýkora was discovered her DNA was found on his fingernails. In 2005, despite her ludicrous claims of innocence, Jaroslava Fabiánová was sentenced to life in prison. She was only the third woman in the history of the Czech Republic to be sentenced to life.

Jaroslava Fabiánová was described as intelligent by the authorities after her conviction and she gave a confident (if futile) performance in court. Experts judged her to be egocentric and suffering from various personality disorders. You could argue that Jaroslava Fabiánová, like Aileen Wuornos, was a financially motivated killer. However, Jaroslava Fabiánová seemed to take more pleasure in the act of killing than Wuornos. She was certainly more gruesome in her methods too.

THOMAS LANCASTER was born in the 17th century in Ashford. Little is known about his upbringing, but it is speculated that his fascination with toxic substances began at an early age. As an adult, he worked as an apothecary, a profession that granted him access to a wide range of poisonous substances, which he employed with deadly intent. Lancaster's method of choice was poison, a weapon that allowed him to hide in plain sight, waiting for the perfect moment to strike. His victims were often unsuspecting individuals, including family members, friends, and even business associates.

What made his crimes even more sinister was his mastery of manipulation. Lancaster would weave intricate narratives, convincing those around him that his victims' deaths were mere accidents or natural occurrences, thus allowing him to evade suspicion for an extended period. During his reign of terror, Lancaster claimed numerous victims through his calculated acts of poisoning. His preferred poison was arsenic, a deadly substance that could be administered in various ways, including mixing it in food and drink. His choice of target was often those closest to him, such as wives, children, and relatives who stood in the way of his personal gain or who he deemed as a threat to his secrets.

Despite Lancaster's cunning and ability to manipulate those around him, his reign of terror eventually came to an end. A combination of suspicious deaths, rumors, and the diligence of law enforcement led to an investigation into his activities. It was during this investigation that the true extent of his crimes began to surface, revealing a web of deceit and death that sent shockwaves throughout the community.

MINNIE DEAN was born in Greenock, Scotland in 1884. At some point she moved to New Zealand and lived with her two children. Minnie claimed to be a widow but actual evidence for this is scant. In 1872, Minnie married Charles Dean. The couple dabbled in various things like farming but money was tight and life was not easy. To make money, Minnie turned to taking in unwanted children who were up for adoption. This was known as baby farming.

Baby farming flourished in this era because it was considered to be a great sin in society for an unmarried woman to have a child. Abortion was dangerous and contraception was not widespread. As a consequence there were always plenty of unwanted illegitimate babies who needed care until a permanent home could be found for them. Sadly, while most of the 'baby farming' women who took in children were kind and dutiful there were some dreadful true crime cases around the world of women who saw baby farming strictly as a means to make money and viewed the children and infants as expendable if they cut into profit margins. Tragically, it seems that Minnie Dean was of this notorious and awful ilk.

There were soon a number of cases where infants and children under Minnie Dean's care died of illness or vanished. This was judged to have gone beyond what you might expect as normal (in those it was sadly not uncommon for infants and children to die of illnesses and diseases which would be treatable or prevented today). Local whispers soon began to suspect Minnie Dean of foul play in her baby farming duties.

One of the salient problems with baby farming in New Zealand was that those who took in children didn't have to keep official records of who they had taken in. This obviously meant that it was difficult to keep track of deaths and disappearances. In 1895, a woman named Jane Hornsby visited Minnie Dean with some police constables and demanded to know where her granddaughter Eva was. Dean had been looking after Eva. However, although clothes belonging to Eva were found at Minnie Dean's house there was no sign of the child. Minnie Dean now had a lot of explaining to do. She was in big trouble.

Minnie Dean was arrested on suspicion of murder and her garden was dug up. The garden had some grisly secrets. There were three bodies buried. One was the missing Eva. The other victims were a one-year girl and a three year-old boy. Eva had been suffocated while one of the babies had been sedated with laudanum. There was also evidence of morphine in two of the infants and morphine was found in the Dean house. The cause of death in the third baby could not be established.

At the trial, Minnie Dean argued that the deaths were of natural causes or accidents and she had tried to hide them because she knew people would wrongly assume she was killing infants to save money. Dean insisted that she had always done her best to look after the children in her care and was most definitely not a child killer. These arguments were clearly not persuasive because she was found guilty of murder and sentenced to death. Minnie Dean is the only woman ever to be hung in New Zealand. She was hanged at the Invercargill gaol. Given that New Zealand has long since abandoned the death penalty, Minnie Dean will forever remain the only female criminal to be hung in that nation.

Before she died, Minnie Dean wrote a long account in which she said the other children who went missing in her care were secretly found families who didn't want their identity to be known. The police begged to differ and thought that Minnie Dean probably killed more infants than they ever managed to find. Minnie Dean's husband was not implicated in the murders and set free after questioning. It transpired that Minnie Dean had suspiciously banned her husband from doing any gardening. He was completely in the dark about what was buried out there.

It's hard to say how many infants and children Minnie Dean really killed but it's probably a lot more than three. Minnie Dean is known as The Southland Witch in New Zealand. There is a wild-flower in Southland known as a Minnie Dean. Should this flower sprout in your garden it is said to signify doom and bad luck. Legend has it that flowers still refuse to grow on land that once belonged to Minnie Dean.

MARIE ROBARDS was born in 1977. At the age of 16, in Fort Worth, Texas, she stole barium acetate from her chemistry class and used it to poison her 38 year-old father Steven. This happened in 1993. Barium acetate is the salt of barium (II) and acetic acid. Barium acetate is toxic to humans, but has use in chemistry and manufacturing. Marie laced her father's beans and Tacos with the chemical and he died as a consequence. Her motive for the murder was that she wanted to go and live with her mother. She nearly got away with it too because her father's death was judged to be a heart attack. No one suspected at the time that his daughter had poisoned him.

It was only many months later that Marie's crime came to light. She confessed the murder to a friend named Stacey and her friend went to a school counselor. The counselor then went to the police. The authorities did an examination and proved that Mr Robards had been poisoned. Marie, now 18 years-old, was arrested in 1994. Marie had no choice but to confess. She was sentenced to 27 years in prison in 1995. Her background was complex in that her parents had divorced when she was 3. She had lived with her mother and stepfather but left that home when she found out her stepfather was cheating on her mother. Marie lived with her grandparents for a time and then moved in with her father.

Marie was desperate to go and live with her mother again but her mother and stepmother would not allow this. Marie then came up with the plan of poisoning her father as a means to go and live with her mother again. Marie was tried as an adult at the trial. She was nineteen though (though sixteen when the crime took place). Her defence argued that Marie didn't mean to kill her father and didn't know barium acetate was deadly. They wanted manslaughter. It was a weak argument though which didn't pass much muster. What harmed Marie too was that she had blankly stood and watched paramedics try to save her father without telling them which poison he had been given.

At the trial, Marie did at least show some remorse - breaking down on the stand when she was asked about her father. The prosecution didn't have too much sympathy though. They called her a narcissist and said she hadn't shown much remorse or guilt about the murder until she was caught. In 2003, Marie was released on parole. She now has a new identity and has lived her life out of the public eye.

MARGUERITE MONOVOISON, commonly known as La Voisin, was a notorious figure in 17th century France. Born in 1640, La Voisin was a French fortune teller and alleged black magician who gained infamy as a key figure in the Affair of the Poisons. La Voisin operated in the realm of underground crime in Paris and was involved in various illegal activities, particularly poisoning. She offered her services as a fortune teller, but her real reputation lay in her ability to provide clients with poisoned concoctions, most notably the "inheritance powders." These powders were used by individuals seeking to eliminate rivals, unwanted family members, or spouses for financial gain.

Her clientele allegedly included nobles, members of the French court, and even royal mistresses. It is believed that La Voisin operated a network of practitioners who supplied her with the necessary ingredients for her deadly potions. In 1679, an investigation into the use of poison and witchcraft began, resulting in the arrest of La Voisin and many of her associates. The trial, known as the Affair of the Poisons, shed light on the dark underbelly of French society and revealed the extent of the criminal activities in which La Voisin and her network were involved.

La Voisin was found guilty of witchcraft, poisoning, and performing black masses. She was sentenced to die by burning at the stake. On February 22, 1680, she was executed in public along with several others involved in the Affair of the Poisons. The case of Marguerite Monvoisin, or La Voisin, remains a fascinating and disturbing episode in French history, shedding light on the widespread belief in witchcraft, sorcery, and the use of poison during the 17th century.

FELIICITAS SANCHEZ AGUILLON was born in Cerro Azul, Veracruz, Mexico in 1890. Her terrible infamy lent her a number of titles - the most common of which are The Female Ripper of Colonia Roma and The Human Crusher of Little Angels. As a young woman she became a nurse although she was not the most maternal of people. She got married and had twin daughters but she was so indifferent to her children she arranged to have them adopted.

Aguillón eventually moved to Mexico City where she began

performing illegal abortions and got involved in the baby farming trade. Any babies that she couldn't get any money for she simply killed. She would drug or strangle the unwanted babies and then dump them in a river or sewer. The babies in her care were treated abominably. She made them sleep on the floor and fed them food that had gone off. They were given cold baths.

The awful crimes of Aguillón were uncovered in 1941 when the building in the Roma neighbourhood where she was based began to experience problems with its drains. Plumbers were sent to rectify the problem and they found things that were grisly and disturbing beyond words. In the pipe they found rotted meat and greased and bloodied rags. They also found a human skull that belonged to a baby. Aguillón is believed to have murdered between forty and fifty babies.

She was able to keep her wicked scheme secret for as long as she did because one of her accomplices was a plumber. In the end though the drains simply became too clogged. Neighbours are said to have become suspicious of Aguillón because a thick pungent black smoke would sometimes come from her rooms. This was clearly a result of her burning the bodies of her victims. Aguillón would sometimes chop the babies up after she had killed them and hide them on garbage dumps.

When the police searched the rooms of Felícitas Sánchez Aguillón they found a number of religious artifacts and photographs of children. She had fled with a lover but thankfully was captured a day later. Felícitas Sánchez Aguillón was found to be a delusional woman who seemed to think she was on some sort of religious mission. She was clearly not the full shilling. Aguillón retreated into a childlike state in custody as the investigation developed.

It was said that Aguillón had some baby adoption clients who were famous and involved in politics. The authorities were eager to get these names but Aguillón committed suicide by an overdose before the full details of her baby farming business were gathered. She was 50 years old. Aguillón had another daughter and husband by the time of her death. Her husband was convicted of being an accomplice and her daughter was placed in foster care. By any standards, Felícitas Sánchez Aguillón was one of the most heartless killers imaginable.

The story of LOCUSTA, the Roman Poisoner is shrouded in mystery and legend. Centuries later, Locusta's notoriety lives on, having become a symbol of the dark arts of assassination. Her name has become synonymous with poison, a deadly tool wielded by those seeking to eliminate their enemies discreetly and without a trace. But who was Locusta, the woman behind the poisoner's veil? What led her to embrace such a nefarious profession, and how did she become so renowned for her poisoned concoctions?

Historical records paint a fragmented picture of Locusta's life, but what is known is both intriguing and disturbing. Born in Gaul during the reign of Emperor Claudius, she initially worked as a herbalist, acquiring knowledge of plants and their properties. It was this very knowledge that would later serve as her gateway into the dark world of poison. Locusta's infamy began to take root during the reign of Emperor Nero, a tyrant known for his cruelty and paranoia.

His reign was marked by political intrigue and the elimination of rivals, which created an environment ripe for the likes of Locusta. Recognising her expertise, Nero enlisted her services, seeking her assistance in disposing of those who posed a threat to his rule. Under Nero's patronage, Locusta refined her skills, experimenting with various toxic substances and creating lethal potions. Her methods were not limited to poisons derived from plants; she also delved into the world of venomous creatures, extracting toxins from snakes and scorpions. Locusta's knowledge grew, and her reputation as a master poisoner spread throughout Rome.

Her most notorious act came in the year 54 AD when Nero ordered her to assassinate Britannicus, his stepbrother and potential rival to the throne. Locusta concocted a poison so potent that it killed Britannicus within moments, a death that sent shockwaves through Rome. This successful mission solidified Locusta's status as one of the most feared and sought-after poisoners of her time. But Locusta's reign of terror was not destined to last. In 55 AD, a new Emperor, Galba, rose to power and sought to purge Nero's allies. Locusta, along with many others, was apprehended and sentenced to death. However, fate intervened, and Galba, recognising her unique skills, instead ordered her to train others in the art of poisoning. Thus, Locusta's expertise was passed down to future generations, ensuring her dark legacy would live on.

JIM JONES, born James Warren Jones, was an American cult leader who gained notoriety for leading the Peoples Temple. He was born on May 13, 1931, in Indiana, and died on November 18, 1978. Jones started the Peoples Temple in the 1950s, promoting a mixture of political activism, religious teachings, and social justice. However, as the years went on, Jones' behavior became increasingly authoritarian, nutty, and manipulative. In 1973, Jones relocated the Peoples Temple to Guyana in South America, establishing a settlement called Jonestown. Members were isolated from the outside world, and Jones held a strong grip on their lives, demanding absolute loyalty and submission.

Tragically, on November 18, 1978, a mass murder-suicide occurred in Jonestown. Influenced by Jones, over 900 members, including children, died after consuming a cyanide-laced grape-flavored drink, while others were shot or forced to commit suicide. It remains one of the largest mass casualty incidents in modern history. The events in Jonestown shocked the world, highlighting the dangers of unchecked power and the vulnerability of individuals susceptible to manipulation by charismatic leaders. It also led to increased scrutiny of cults and the need for regulations to protect vulnerable individuals from exploitation.

The phrase 'drinking the Kool-Aid' has long since entered the lexicon of American culture thanks to the 1978 Jonestown Massacre where the cult followers of Jim Jones committed suicide in Guyana. They are alleged to have drunk poisoned Kool-Aid - although many contend this is an urban myth and they actually used another soft drink. Anyway, to this day, anyone who is deemed to be gullible or dangerously misguided is still sometimes accused of 'drinking the Kool-Aid'. Kool-Aid is an American brand of flavored drink mix owned by Kraft Heinz based in Chicago, Illinois. The powder form was created by Edwin Perkins in 1927 based upon a liquid concentrate called Fruit Smack. You can buy Kool-Aid online outside the United States. It's a fizzy drink which you mix from a sachet.

MARY BLANDLY was born in 1720 in Henley-on-Thames, England to a wealthy family. She was well-educated and considered a beauty in her youth. In 1746, she met Captain William Henry Cranstoun and they began a secret relationship as her father disapproved of him. In 1751, Mary's father grew ill and she took on the role of his caregiver. During this time, she began adding small amounts of arsenic to his food and drinks, allegedly at the urging of her lover. Her father's health continued to decline and he eventually died in 1751. Suspicion fell on Mary when a doctor discovered high levels of arsenic in her father's body. Mary was arrested and her trial drew national attention. Despite her claims of innocence and her lover's attempts to save her, she was found guilty and sentenced to death by hanging. She was executed in 1752, but her case has continued to capture public interest and has been retold in various forms of media. It remains a controversial and often debated case in history.

LUCRETIA BORGIA (1480-1519) was an Italian noblewoman and a member of the notorious Borgia family the Renaissance period. She was the daughter of Pope VI and his mistress Vannozza deiattanei. Lucretia is often depicted in history as a femme fatale, involved in numerous scandals and conspiracies. Lucretia Borgia was married three times, in strategic alliances arranged by her father for the benefit of their family's political ambitions. Her first marriage was to Giovanni Sforza, which ultimately ended in annulment due to political reasons. She then married Alfonso of Aragon, who was later murdered by her brother Cesare to secure a new alliance. Lucretia's third marriage was to Alfonso d'Este, becoming the Duchess of Ferrara.

Throughout her life, Lucretia was surrounded by rumors of incestuous relationships with her father and brother, as well as her involvement in poisonings and political assassinations. However, it should be noted that these claims were mostly made by their enemies and may have been exaggerated or unfounded. She was often portrayed as a cunning and manipulative figure, using her sexuality to advance the interests of her family. Despite the controversial reputation surrounding her, Lucretia Borgia was also known as a patron of the arts. She supported many artists of the time, including the painter Titian, and was a knowledgeable collector of books and manuscripts. Lucretia Borgia died in childbirth in 1519 at the age of 39. Her life and reputation continue to be subjects of fascination in popular culture, with numerous books, plays, and movies depicting her as a femme fatale and a symbol of power and intrigue.

STEPHEN PORT is a rapist and killer who murdered four men in London from 2014 to 2015. He would drug them with GBH (gamma-Hydroxybutyric acid - known as a 'date rape' drug). Three of the victims were disposed of in a graveyard by Port. He was given life in prison. Stephen Port, who worked as a chef in a bus depot, once appeared on televison as a kitchen assistant in the popular BBC show Masterchef. The BBC have obviously now edited him out of that episode. Port was a very dangerous and ruthless man. He was overwhelmed by his fantasy of having sex with victims who were inert or helpless (this is a common heme in serial killers). Port even faked suicide notes for some of his victims and this made the police slow in connecting the deaths. Port met his victims through online dating apps and this case led to some understandable concern over the safety of such apps.

Port was born in Essex in 1975. He went to art college but dropped out - eventually becoming a chef. Port was considered to be an odd character by those that knew him as a young man. He always felt like an outsider and suffered from bullying as a child. Port lived alone in a flat and began to create a sort of fictitious fantasy life to escape from the rather mundane reality of his real circumstances. Because he was bald, Port would wear an elaborate blonde wig in his online photographs to make himself seem younger and more attractive on online dating sites. Port only came out as gay in his mid twenties so clearly struggled with his sexuality as a very young man.

When he spoke to people online or wrote a profile, Port would make things up to make himself seem more interesting. He would do things like pretend that he'd been to Oxford University or served in the Royal Navy. Port's first victim was Anthony Walgate, 23, a fashion student originally from Hull. Walgate was an escort and Port arranged to meet him by posing as a client with lots of money. Port drugged and killed Walgate and then dumped the body outside his flat. Port then called the police and reported that a man had collapsed outside of his building. Amazingly, this ruse actually worked and Port didn't attract any suspicion.

Port's three other victims were Gabriel Kovari, 22, Daniel Whitworth, 21, and Jack Taylor, 25. Port put the bodies of these victims in a local graveyard - where they were of course eventually discovered by members of the public. Port placed a fake suicide note on Whitworth which stated that Whitworth had killed Kovari. It was all a crude deception plan by Port to mask his own depravity. Incredibly, the original inquest returned open verdicts on the deaths of these men. The gay community were unhappy at the way the Met handled this case because it seemed obvious to them that a serial killer was at work and targeting gay men but the police seemed very slow to deduce this for themselves.

The famalies of the victims were also very unhappy with the police handling of this case. It transpired that the police had not even had the suicide note found on Whitworth submitted to handwriting experts or the family to test its veracity. The family of Jack Taylor found it strange too that Jack was very anti-drugs but was found with a potent cocktail of drugs in his system. When the family of Daniel Whitworth contacted the police eleven days after his death to ask how the investigation was going they were amazed and angered to learn that was no police investigation at all and the Met had seemingly washed their hands of the affair.

Thankfully, CCTV of Stephen Port with one of the victims eventually turned up and he was able to be linked with these crimes. The police said he was a very dangerous and cold hearted man. Mr Justice Openshaw said At Port's trial - "The murders were committed as part of a persistent course of conduct of the defendant surreptitiously drugging these young men so that he could penetrate them while they were unconscious. A significant degree of planning went into obtaining the drugs in advance and in luring the victims to his flat.

"Having killed them by administering an overdose, he dragged them out into the street in one case, or took them to the churchyard in the other cases, and abandoned their bodies in a manner which robbed them of their dignity, and thereby greatly increased the distress of their loving families. I have no doubt that the seriousness of the offending is so exceptionally high that the whole-life order is justified; indeed it is required. The sentence therefore upon the counts of murder is a sentence of life imprisonment. I decline to set a minimum term. The result is a whole-life sentence and the defendant will die in prison."

Police officers involved in this case faced disciplinary action and the families of the victims launched a civil suit. There had definitely been mistakes and the police were clearly not sensitive enough to the concerns and anguish of the victims families and the gay community. The investigation was not the finest hour of the Met. At the very least though Stephen Port was in prison and no danger to anyone anymore. Port was an exceptionally devious and heartless killer who would almost certainly have killed others if he hadn't been captured.

MARSHALL APPLEWHITE, born on May 17, 1931, in Spur, Texas, was a controversial figure and the co-founder of the Heaven's Gate religious cult. He gained notoriety for his role in leading the cult and orchestrating a mass suicide event in 1997. Applewhite initially started out as a music teacher but later became involved in religious and philosophical teachings. He teamed up with Bonnie Nettles, and together they formed the belief system that would become the foundation of Heaven's Gate. They believed in the existence of extraterrestrial beings and the idea of ascension to a higher level of existence.

Applewhite and Nettles attracted followers who believed in their teachings, and the group adopted a strict and isolated lifestyle. In 1997, they perceived the approach of a comet called Hale-Bopp as a sign to leave their earthly bodies and join the extraterrestrial realm. On March 26, 1997, 39 members of the cult, including Applewhite, died by consuming a lethal mixture of alcohol and drugs in a mass suicide event. Suffice to say, Applewhite was a deluded, manipulative, and in the end highly dangerous man. The end result was an awful tragedy and highlighted the danger of becoming brainwashed by cult groups.

MILKA PAVOVIC was born in Kokinac, Kingdom of Croatia-Slavonia in 1905. Pavlović was born into a peasant family and as a young woman got married and worked as a milkmaid (basically someone who milks cows). Her husband was named Rade Pavlović. Milka Pavlović was a miserable looking woman who seemed to have a permanent scowl. She wasn't very popular in the community. In 1934 Pavlović purchased some arsenic for what she claimed was a problem with rats. The recipient of this arsenic was not rats but her husband Rade. She put the poison in his food and he expired fairly quickly thereafter.

According to Medical News Today - 'The symptoms of arsenic poisoning can be acute, or severe and immediate, or chronic, where damage to health is experienced over a longer period. This will often depend on the method of exposure. A person who has swallowed arsenic may show signs and symptoms within 30 minutes. These may include: drowsiness, headaches, confusion, severe diarrhoea. As the arsenic poisoning progresses, the patient may start experiencing convulsions, and their fingernail pigmentation may change. Signs and symptoms associated with more severe cases of arsenic poisoning are: a metallic taste in the mouth and garlicky breath, excess saliva, problems swallowing, blood in the urine, cramping muscles, hair loss, stomach cramps, convulsions, excessive sweating. Arsenic poisoning typically affects the skin, liver, lungs, and kidneys. In the final stage, symptoms include seizures and shock. This could lead to a coma or death.'

Rade's death was not deemed especially suspicious at the time but Milka Pavlović rather pushed her luck thereafter with her rampant arsenic poisoning. She poisoned dozens of relatives and also servants in the house of the family in which she worked. The final straw turned out to be the death of a blacksmith. He had been suddenly taken ill with dreadful stomach pains and died as a result - despite being a healthy and strong man only days before. Locals noted that the death of the blacksmith was suspiciously similar to the sudden and unexpected demise of Rade - the husband of Milka Pavlović.

Milka Pavlović was arrested and eventually confessed that she poisoned all these people for financial gain. Some exhumations took place to establish her guilt. There were six victims (that is to say people who died) of Milka Pavlović in all but it could have been far worse because she attempted to poison dozens of other people who somehow manage to survive and eventually recover. At the trial it transpired that Pavlović put the arsenic in salt and biscuits. She had even planned to poison a two year-old child to seize an inheritance but (fortunately for the child) this wicked scheme was foiled when Milka Pavlović was arrested. Milka Pavlović was executed by hanging in 1935. She was thirty years-old at the time of her death.

9 798223 559702